FORT WORTH

WHERE THE BEST BEGINS

Modern cattle drive near downtown Fort Worth

FORT WORTH

WHERE THE BEST BEGINS

KATHRYN HOPPER • WORTH S. WREN JR.

This book was produced in cooperation with the Fort Worth Chamber of Commerce. Cherbo Publishing Group gratefully acknowledges their important contribution to *Fort Worth: Where the Best Begins*.

cherbo publishing group, inc.

president	JACK C. CHERBO
executive vice president	ELAINE HOFFMAN
editorial director	CHRISTINA M. BEAUSANG
managing feature editor	MARGARET L. MARTIN
senior profiles editor	J. KELLEY YOUNGER
feature editors	JO ELLEN KRUMM KRISTINA SAUERWEIN
profiles editors	BENJAMIN PROST LIZA YETENEKIAN SMITH
contributing editors	B. D. CAMPBELL TERRI JONISCH ERICA RHEINSCHILD
associate editor	SYLVIA EMRICH-TOMA
proofreaders	ELIZABETH FENNER JENNY KORNFELD
profiles writers	LINDA CHASE SYLVIA EMRICH-TOMA TERRI JONISCH TERRAN LAMP MARY MARSHALL STEFANIE SPIKELL
creative director	PERI A. HOLGUIN
senior designer	THEODORE E. YEAGER
designer	NELSON CAMPOS
senior photo editor	WALTER MLADINA
photo editor	DAVID ZANZINGER
digital color specialist	ART VASQUEZ
sales administrator	JOAN K. BAKER
profile services supervisor	PATRICIA DE LEONARD
profile services coordinators	LESLIE E. SHAW KENYA HICKS
administrative assistants	JUDY ROBITSCHEK BILL WAY
southwest regional manager	JOHN HECKER
publisher's representative	JOHN TEW

Cherbo Publishing Group, Inc.
Encino, California 91316

Printed in Canada
By Friesens

Subsidiary Production Office
Santa Rosa, CA, USA
888.340.6049

Library of Congress Cataloging-in-Publication data
Hopper, Kathryn and Worth S. Wren Jr.
A pictorial guide highlighting Fort Worth's economic and social advantages.
Library of Congress Control Number: 2006932540
ISBN 978-1-882933-76-1

Visit the CPG Web site at www.cherbopub.com.

NASCAR tire check at the Texas Motor Speedway

TABLE OF CONTENTS

COMPANIES & ORGANIZATIONS PROFILED

The following organizations have made a valuable commitment to the quality of this publication. The Fort Worth Chamber of Commerce gratefully acknowledges their participation in *Fort Worth: Where the Best Begins*.

BUSINESS VISIONARIES

The following companies and organizations are recognized as innovators in their fields and have played a prominent role in this publication, as they have in the state.

Alcon®

Alcon, Inc.
6201 South Freeway, Fort Worth, TX 76134
Contact: Doug MacHatton, Vice President, Investor Relations and Strategic Corporate Communications
Phone: 817-293-0450 / Fax: 817-615-4607
E-mail: doug.machatton@alconlabs.com
Web site: www.alconinc.com/us

Citizens NATIONAL BANK

Citizens National Bank
Corporate Office
2720 West 7th Street, Fort Worth, TX 76107
Contact: Raymond G. Dickerson, President and CEO
Phone: 817-731-1444 / Fax: 817-738-7411
E-mail: raygd@citizensnationalbank.com
Web site: www.citizensnationalbank.com
"Real People. Real Solutions."

CRESCENT®

Crescent Real Estate Equities Company
777 Main Street, Suite 2100, Fort Worth, TX 76102
Contact: John C. Goff, Vice Chairman and Chief Executive Officer
Phone: 817-321-2100 / Fax: 817-321-2060
Web site: www.crescent.com
"Distinctly Different"

DFW

DALLAS/FORT WORTH
INTERNATIONAL AIRPORT

Dallas/Fort Worth International Airport
3200 East Airfield Drive, DFW Airport, TX 75261
Contact: Jeff Fegan, CEO
Phone: 972-574-8888
E-mail: AirportInfoCenter@dfwairport.com
Web site: www.dfwairport.com
"The World Connected"

DFB PHARMACEUTICALS™

DFB Pharmaceuticals, Inc.
3909 Hulen Street, Fort Worth, TX 76107
Contact: Douglas L. Cook, Director of Corporate Administration
Phone: 817-900-4000 / Fax: 817-900-4101
E-mail: doug.cook@dfb.com
Web site: www.dfb.com
"A Specialty Pharmaceutical Company"

National FARM·LIFE

National Farm Life Insurance Company
6001 Bridge Street, Fort Worth, TX 76112
Contact: J. D. "Chip" Davis, President and CEO
Phone: 800-772-7557 or 817-451-9550 / Fax: 817-451-6358
E-mail: customer_service@nflic.com
Web site: www.nflic.com
"Providing Security for the Future"

OmniAmerican Bank
P. O. Box 150099, Fort Worth, TX 76108
Contact: Ginger Johnson, Director of Client Managers
Phone: 817-367-4663 / Fax: 817-367-5683
E-mail: Ginger.Johnson@OmniAmerican.com
Web site: www.OmniAmerican.com

University of North Texas Health Science Center
3500 Camp Bowie Boulevard, Fort Worth, TX 76107
Contact: Jean Tips, Assistant Vice President,
Marketing and Communications
Phone: 817-735-2000
E-mail: jtips@hsc.unt.edu
Web site: www.hsc.unt.edu

XTO Energy Inc.
810 Houston Street, Fort Worth, TX 76102
Phone: 817-870-2800 / Fax: 817-870-1671
Web site: www.xtoenergy.com

Doug Harmon, president of the Fort Worth Convention and Visitors Bureau

Leddy's Ranch, Sundance Square

Van Cliburn, the inspiration behind the Van Cliburn International Piano Competition held in Fort Worth since 1962, surrounded by six finalists selected after more than two weeks of thrilling performances

FOREWORD

Welcome to the best of the West—Fort Worth, Texas. Here we proudly honor our Texas heritage, but we also embrace creativity and the fine arts. We have a comfortable and cultured way of life.

As a concert pianist touring the world, I am always happy to come home to Fort Worth. The values of my hometown, the friendly people, and their commitment to the arts make Fort Worth the perfect venue for the Van Cliburn International Piano Competition. Every four years since 1962, the people of Fort Worth have welcomed the most outstanding young pianists from around the world.

Music and art are extremely important here, as detailed in *Fort Worth: Where the Best Begins*. As part of an ongoing commitment to our cultural life, we now have the Nancy Lee and Perry R. Bass Performing Arts Center, a world-class venue for the Fort Worth Symphony, Fort Worth Opera, Texas Ballet Theater, and other forms of music and art. It is the home of the international piano competition, sponsored by the Van Cliburn Foundation, which also offers a concert series and other programs for the people of North Texas. We are happy to share the joy of great music with the people of Fort Worth.

As I look out on the downtown skyline from my home, I note the progress of the past half-century. We have built many impressive commercial and residential complexes, upgraded our museums, gardens, and theaters, and preserved the best of the past. As this book observes, Fort Worth is headquarters to many national corporations. Our community has created jobs as well as business and educational opportunities. Our remarkable air and land transportation hub is convenient not only for artists flying in and out, but also for businesspeople and cargo to be on their way efficiently. We are positioned for continued growth, and we welcome businesses, individuals, and families who want to share in the prosperity.

Above everything else, it is the people that make Fort Worth great. Not only do they support our young musicians, but they also support each other with their gracious hospitality, refinement, and largesse. I am more than proud to call Fort Worth my home.

Van Cliburn

Van Cliburn

FORT WORTH TIMELINE

1849 1878

The Tarantula Train, a late-19th-century locomotive

1849 Major Ripley A. Arnold and a troop of soldiers set up a fort on the Trinity River to protect early settlers from Native American attacks. The fort is named for Major General William J. Worth, a hero of the Mexican War.

1853 The U.S. Army abandons Fort Worth for new posts further west, and pioneer settlers already in the area claim it as their permanent home.

1854 The first public school in town is established by John Peter Smith in an abandoned army hospital. Smith's importance in the community earns him the nickname the "Father of Fort Worth."

1860 After a long and bitter fight known as the County Seat War, Fort Worth becomes the home of government for Tarrant County.

1866 Fort Worth, a stopping point for cowboys herding cattle along the Chisholm Trail, earns the nickname "Cowtown." Growth and prosperity as a cattle trading center help the town recover from post–Civil War shortages.

1873 The Texas and Pacific Railroad agrees to a charter that will bring a railroad through town.

1873 W. P. Burts is elected Fort Worth's first mayor.

1876 The tracks in Fort Worth are completed and the Texas and Pacific Railway arrives, turning the city into a transit point for cattle shipments and wholesale trade.

Yuma Stage Line, 1878

1878 The Yuma Stage Line makes regular stops in Fort Worth, which will become the eastern terminus for the route to Yuma, Arizona.

1883 Fort Worth's first hospital, the Missouri Pacific Hospital, is built to serve the health care needs of railroad workers. In 1930 its name is changed to St. Joseph Hospital.

1884 Local businessmen establish Fort Worth National Bank, originally named Tidball, Van Zandt, and Company.

1889 As part of the town's strategy for continued growth and commercial expansion, the Texas Spring Palace opens as an educational, cultural, and entertainment center designed to attract both settlers and investors.

1892 The State of Texas grants a charter to establish the Fort Worth Public Library Association, which is devoted to the "accumulation of paintings and artistic work." Many years later the Modern Art Museum of Fort Worth (the Modern) is a thriving cultural landmark.

1896 1917 1922

1896 The first livestock show in Fort Worth is held near Marine Creek. The event later becomes known as the Fat Stock Show, a world-famous livestock exhibition and rodeo.

1903 Attracted by financial incentives, railroads, and abundant cattle, the Armour and Swift meat packing companies decide to open plants in Fort Worth.

1908 The Cowtown Coliseum, completed at a cost of $250,000, holds the country's first exhibition cattle roundup conducted under a roof.

1908 The Southwestern Baptist Theological Seminary is established. It will become one of the largest seminaries in the world.

1909 The Fort Worth Zoo opens.

1911 A dam constructed on the West Fork River creates Lake Worth, a reliable water supply and at the time the largest municipal water-supply reservoir in Texas.

1917 Construction of Camp Bowie, named after the Alamo hero James Bowie, begins three miles west of downtown. The camp trains the 36th Infantry Division for 10 months before the soldiers are shipped to France.

1917 Oil gushes from a well on the McCleskey Farm west of Fort Worth, bringing economic prosperity and helping to meet the fuel demands of World War I.

Student pilot with instructor at Meacham Field, January 1942

1918 The Southwestern Exposition and Fat Stock Show holds the world's first indoor rodeo—increasing the event's attendance considerably and becoming the high point of the year for thousands of people.

1920 Five working refineries tap Fort Worth's underground oil reserves, making the city a center for oil activity and turning many ranchers and farmers into millionaires. Luxury homes and office buildings follow the newly found wealth.

1922 Fort Worth resident and newspaper owner Amon G. Carter Sr. establishes WBAP, Fort Worth's first radio station, which will become one of the few 50,000-watt clear-channel stations in the country. It is also the first radio station to broadcast livestock market reports and weekly church services.

1925 The Fort Worth Municipal Airport is established, and two years later is named Meacham Field after the town's former mayor.

1930 The Fort Worth Panthers (precursor of the Cats) baseball team wins the Texas League Crown.

1936 The Texas Centennial Frontier—celebrating the 100-year anniversary of the Republic of Texas—is held in Fort Worth. Sponsored by Amon G. Carter Sr. at a cost of $5 million, it depicts life on the frontier.

1941 Fort Worth Museum of Science and History opens; it is the first children's museum in Texas and one of the first such museums in the country.

FORT WORTH TIMELINE

1941

1941 The Consolidated Aircraft Company announces the construction of a $10 million plant near Fort Worth to build four-motor bombers. The main building of the factory covers 30 acres.

1942 After the attack on Pearl Harbor in December 1941, Tarrant Field is assigned to the Army Air Forces Flying Training Command. The base serves as a pilot transition school and aircraft factory throughout World War II and is named Carswell Air Force Base in 1948.

1948 The first commercial television station in Texas—WBAP-TV—begins in Fort Worth. The station's first broadcast is of a speech given by President Harry Truman.

1956 Elvis Presley entertains 7,000 fans at the Cowtown Coliseum.

1958 The Fort Worth Rodeo becomes the first rodeo to receive live national television coverage, on NBC-TV. Roy Rogers and Dale Evans host the show.

1959 The Fort Worth Independent School District is chosen as the home of a special laboratory for superior science students that will be funded by grants from the National Institutes of Health.

1962 Decreased demand for its products forces Armour and Company to close its meat packing plant.

1962 The first Van Cliburn International Piano Competition is held in Fort Worth.

1971

1971 Fort Worth's cattle industry takes another hit when Swift and Company, one of the nation's largest meat packers, closes its plant.

1973 The Dallas/Fort Worth International Airport opens. It is the largest airport in the United States at the time.

1984 Texas-born George Strait's country-western song "Does Fort Worth Ever Cross Your Mind?" strikes a chord with millions of listeners, tops the *Billboard* chart, then wins the Country Music Association's Album of the Year award in 1985.

1986 Downtown Fort Worth, a victim of urban decay, gets its first public improvement district. Sundance Square will develop into a vibrant 20-block entertainment and commercial area featuring shops, restaurants, nightclubs, theaters, and high-rise living.

1991 The United States Bureau of Engraving and Printing holds the official opening of its Western Currency Facility in Fort Worth, chosen from 80 cities as the site for printing U.S. currency.

1992 The Fort Worth Zoo reopens after numerous improvements throughout. Attendance reaches one million visitors that year.

1998

1998 Bass Performance Hall opens, the crown jewel of the downtown revitalization project. It is the permanent home of the Fort Worth Symphony Orchestra, Texas Ballet Theater, Fort Worth Opera, and Van Cliburn International Piano Competition.

1998 Fort Worth is ranked number one on *Money* magazine's list of the South's Most Livable Places.

2000 A classification F-2 tornado tears through downtown, causing property damage valued at more than $500 million and claiming five lives.

2001 The Amon Carter Museum opens after a $39 million expansion that triples its exhibit space. The magnificent new museum houses Carter's large collection of sculptures by Frederic Remington and Charles M. Russell, as well as 19th- and 20th-century paintings, photographs, and graphic arts.

2002 2003

2002 A record 951,000 people attend the Forth Worth Stock Show.

2002 The National Cowgirl Museum and Hall of Fame relocates from Hereford to a new facility in Fort Worth's Cultural District. The museum is the only one in the world that honors the pioneer women of the American West.

2003 Fort Worth Convention Center gets a $75 million renovation, making the facility a premier 21st-century venue for shows and exhibits.

2003 The Fort Worth City Council adopts a Master Plan for an 88-mile stretch of the Trinity River. The plan calls for expanded parks, trails, water recreation, environmental preservation, residential development, and commercial support in the heart of the city.

2004 By sustaining a high quality of life for its citizens and maximizing the value of the community's assets, Fort Worth earns recognition as one of America's Most Livable Communities by Partners for Livable Communities.

2005 Nearly six million passengers travel through Dallas/Fort Worth International Airport, making it the sixth-busiest airport in the world by number of passengers.

2006 Dallas/Fort Worth International Airport is named "The Best Cargo Airport in the World" by *Air Cargo World* magazine in its Air Cargo Excellence Survey.

Dallas/Fort Worth International Airport

Sundance Square

PART ONE
THE GOOD LIFE: A FORT WORTH OVERVIEW

HALTOM'S
3rd St
Sundance Square

Opposite page: Downtown, a gleaming skyscraper towers over historic Sundance Square, where Texas country music radio station KFWR 95.9 the Ranch broadcasts from its glassed-in studio. This page, below left: Billy Bob's Texas, billed as the world's largest honky-tonk, has music and dancing for all. This page, below right: Longhorns can be seen daily on cattle drives.

FORT WORTH: CITY WITHOUT LIMITS

Quality of Life

Cowboys and culture. Remington and Rembrandt. Willie Nelson and Wolfgang Mozart. Baseball and ballet. From down-home country to upscale cosmopolitan, Fort Worth has it all.

The longhorns are on the move in the Stockyards National Historic District, and guitar sounds fill the air at gargantuan Billy Bob's Texas. Western fun abounds in Fort Worth, but that's only part of what this thriving metropolis is all about.

The excitement never stops in this city where the West begins. Here more than half a million people enjoy a great life with affordable homes, safe neighborhoods, quality schools and colleges, abundant outdoor recreation, arts and culture, world-class hospitals, and excellent employment. With hundreds of recreational, cultural, educational, sports, and entertainment choices, people never run out of things to do.

Founded as an Army outpost in 1849, Fort Worth later became a cowtown, a major stop on the famed Chisholm Trail, and a hangout for the infamous Butch Cassidy and the Sundance Kid. Today Fort Worth has grown into a major metropolis with all the amenities of the big city while retaining the friendliness of a small town.

Fort Worth's attractions are easy to find. Three key sections of town are Downtown, with the redeveloped historic section Sundance Square; the Cultural District, with five museums, the Will Rogers Memorial Center, and a musical theater; and the Stockyards District, with the cattle drive, the Cowtown Coliseum, and Billy Bob's Texas. Among other major attractions, the Fort Worth Zoo is south of downtown; the Fort Worth Nature Center and Refuge is northwest; and Ameriquest Field ballpark and Six Flags over Texas theme park are a quick drive to the east.

This page, top right, and opposite page, bottom right: Fort Worth Stockyards is a destination for entertainment, shopping, and a bull-riding challenge. This page, bottom: One of two 48-foot-tall angel sculptures heralds Bass Performance Hall, one of the top performance centers in the nation. It fills an entire square block. Opposite page, top: Sundance Square shines at night, with entertainment, clubs, dining, and shopping. Opposite page, bottom left: A child is fascinated by the Stock Show parade.

Wild West

The Stockyards National Historic District honors Fort Worth's western heritage on the hoof, with twice-daily cattle drives with the Texas longhorn herd. The district includes the Cowtown Coliseum, Stockyards Station, and legendary Billy Bob's Texas. At Billy Bob's, visitors appreciate the establishment's billing as the largest honky-tonk in the world. It has nearly three acres of indoor space to hold more than 6,000 people. A venue for top bands and dancing, it even has an indoor ring for real professional bull-riding.

Other popular attractions include the White Elephant Saloon, which echoes the Wild West with music and dancing, a vast collection of cowboy hats, and, as the name suggests, a collection of elephants.

Children will love finding their way through the Cowtown Cattlepen Maze. Nearby, the Texas Cowboy Hall of Fame salutes the cowboys and cowgirls of the Lone Star State.

Rodeos, parades, and Wild West extravaganzas entertain the crowds here in the Stockyards District. Country-music icon Willie Nelson's famous Fourth of July picnics bring fans by the thousands.

Western heritage extends beyond the district. The National Cowgirl Museum and Hall of Fame, the only center dedicated to women's role in the West, is in the Cultural District. Annie Oakley and country singer Patsy Cline are among the women honored. Visitors can get in touch with their inner cowgirl (or cowboy) with a videotaped ride on the Bucking Bronc.

The National Cowboys of Color Museum and Hall of Fame tells the complete story of the American West from a multicultural perspective. In Forest Park, Log Cabin Village, with authentic pioneer cabins, brings the mid 19th century to life through stories, music, and demonstrations. Cattle Raisers Museum on the western edge of downtown tells the story of the cattle industry in interactive exhibits with hands-on displays.

JUVENILE
SHOE STORE
amc

Top: The landmark Santa Fe Building, most recently the Rail Market, will reopen in spring 2007 as the University of Texas at Arlington/ Fort Worth Higher Education Center. Adjacent to the Intermodal Transportation Center hub for rail and bus service, the facility will offer graduate and continuing education courses. Bottom: The headquarters buildings of Pier 1 Imports (center) and Cash America International (right) are standouts in the Fort Worth skyline.

Thriving Downtown

Downtown maintains Fort Worth's western heritage with Sundance Square, named for the Sundance Kid. The 20-block area of redeveloped and rebuilt buildings, commercial businesses, upscale residences, specialty stores, restaurants, and theaters has become a thriving urban community. It hums at night, too, with coveys of people out and about, enjoying clubs, shows, and restaurants.

A big part of that nightlife is the Nancy Lee and Perry R. Bass Performance Hall. With 2,056 seats, it takes up a full city block. Opened in 1998, it is the permanent home to major performing arts organizations including the Fort Worth Symphony, the Texas Ballet Theater, and the Fort Worth Opera. Bass Hall also stages Broadway shows and appearances by top-name performers. Once every four years, Fort Worth takes center stage in the world of classical music as the famed Van Cliburn International Piano Competition draws top young pianists from around the globe.

Museum Mecca

Fort Worth is a museum mecca, with its own Cultural District that encompasses five museums, a musical theater, and the Will Rogers Memorial Center in a parklike setting with outdoor sculpture. The district, two and a half miles west of downtown, is the third-largest cultural district in the nation.

The Modern Art Museum of Fort Worth moved into its new home in 2002. Renowned architect Tadao Ando designed the stunning glass-walled structure of 53,000 square feet. The grounds also feature a 1.5-acre reflecting pool.

In 2001, the Amon Carter Museum moved into a new building designed by Philip Johnson. With more than 100 works by

MARKET

Cash America International

Frederic Remington and Charles M. Russell, this American art museum has one of the most comprehensive collections by the two greatest artists of the American West. Other American artists displayed include John James Audubon, Georgia O'Keeffe, Winslow Homer, Mary Cassatt, and Grant Wood.

The Kimbell Art Museum houses a world-class collection dating from antiquity to the 20th century. Its Renaissance art and 17th-century European art collections are particularly impressive, with works by Rembrandt and El Greco. Architect Louis Kahn designed the expansive museum structure of 16 vaulted units and 22,000 square feet of gallery space.

Also in the Cultural District is the Fort Worth Museum of Science and History. Its interactive exhibits and IMAX theater make learning come alive for children. The museum is building a new facility scheduled to open in 2009 that will house expanded exhibits and will include a new center for the Cattle Raisers Museum, spotlighting the cattle and ranching industries.

The fifth museum in the district is the National Cowgirl Museum and Hall of Fame, which pays tribute to women of the past and present through films, photographs, and interactive exhibits.

The city has museums beyond the Cultural District. Downtown, the Sid Richardson Collection of Western Art also has an impressive array of works by Remington and Russell.

Two museums focus on industries that shaped Fort Worth. The Stockyards Museum tells the history of the meat-packing industry, the Fort Worth Stockyards Company, and the bustling area once dubbed "Wall Street of the West." The American Airlines C. R. Smith Museum is one of the only museums in the world dedicated to commercial aviation history.

At the Oscar E. Monnig Meteorite Gallery at Texas Christian University (TCU), visitors can view and touch meteorites from the museum's collection of more than 1,000 meteorites that have landed all over the world.

Opposite page: Frederic Remington's *Coming through the Rye* captures the Old West at the Amon Carter Museum, home to one of the largest collections of the works of Remington and Charles Russell. This page, top: The exterior of the National Cowgirl Museum and Hall of Fame features this trompe l'oeil mural by Richard Haas. This page, bottom: The Fort Worth Museum of Science and History's interactive exhibits make learning fun. A new building opens in 2009.

This page: A white tiger makes his home at the Fort Worth Zoo's Asian Falls exhibit. The zoo has more than 400 species housed in special habitats. Opposite page, top left and right: For shopping and dining, Hulen and Ridgmar malls offer hundreds of upscale choices. Opposite page, center right and bottom: Fort Worth offers a wide choice of dining options, from Mexican fare at Joe T. Garcia's on Commerce Street to rooftop dining at Reata above Sundance Square.

Fantastic Zoo

Fort Worth is rightly proud of its nationally ranked zoo. The 68-acre facility has 435 species of animals, birds, and reptiles. The zoo is working with 35 endangered species and supports more than 20 conservation projects around the globe. New at the zoo is the Great Barrier Reef, an aquatic exhibit with three saltwater tanks full of 500 vibrant fish, coral, and sharks. The zoo is also the only one in the nation to house representatives of all four great ape species—gorilla, orangutan, bonobo, and chimpanzee. The zoo's Asian Falls residents include Asian elephants and Indonesian and white tigers and their cubs, while giraffes, rhinos, and ostriches run on the African Savannah.

Shopping and Dining Sensations

From cowboy boots to couture, antiques to autos, Fort Worth entices residents and visitors with a wide variety of shopping options. Sundance Square has many unique specialty shops, plus chic restaurants for refueling during the shopping and touring day. The Stockyards District is the natural spot to stock up on Western wear while enjoying fine dining. Montgomery Street Antiques Mall has more than 100 stalls of antique and unique merchandise.

Fort Worth's sophisticated retail centers include open-air complexes such as Trinity Commons, with its Old World European design, pedestrian-friendly walkways, and central fountain. Chapel Hill Shopping Center sits in the shadow of the Marty Leonard Chapel, designed by famed architect

Fay Jones. It is anchored by HEB's Central Market, an epicurean's delight specializing in gourmet foods, fresh produce, and chef-prepared meals. University Park Village draws upscale shoppers from nearby Texas Christian University. Its more than 30 stores include national retailers as well as local restaurants.

Fort Worth and Tarrant County have some of the region's largest malls, including Hulen Mall, with national stores and more than 120 specialty shops. Newly renovated Ridgmar Mall has separate districts for fashion, sports, and children, and is anchored by Neiman Marcus, Dillard's, Macy's, and JCPenney. In nearby Hurst, gigantic North East Mall features more than 140 specialty shops plus Saks Fifth Avenue, Nordstrom, and other national stores.

Located just north of Dallas/Fort Worth (DFW) International Airport, Grapevine Mills is a bargain-hunters bonanza with more than 150 stores, including many outlets.

Fort Worth has great choices in automotive shopping, too. Toyota of Fort Worth has a 13-acre campus with hundreds of vehicles for sale, and Frank Kent Motor Co., which has been in business for nearly 80 years, has six franchises.

The city has a plethora of restaurants, from fancy dining rooms to tiny hamburger stands. Many of them are basic diners and family restaurants with good food at good prices. Tastes here are international, and include Italian, Greek, Indian, Thai, Vietnamese, Chinese, Japanese, and, of course, Tex-Mex and Mexican.

This page, top left: The Botanic Garden is a haven with 2,500 species in 109 acres. This page, bottom left: Visitors get splashed at Six Flags Hurricane Harbor in nearby Arlington. This page, right: Lewisville Lake, one of 18 lakes in the area, has great fishing. Opposite page: It's easy to get out of the city and enjoy the wide-open spaces and glorious sunsets, such as this one north of Fort Worth.

The Great Outdoors

One of the most exhilarating things about living here is the chance to enjoy the great outdoors, the sun, the sky, the fresh air. With Fort Worth averaging 232 sunny days a year, who can stay indoors? Fair weather abounds.

The long, dusty rides on the Chisholm Trail are over, but miles of urban trails take today's residents and guests near and far. Along the Trinity River, Trinity Trails stretches for 30 miles of paved trails for biking, walking, running, or inline skating. The city's 200 parks cover more than 10,000 acres with wide-open spaces for everyone.

The Botanic Garden south of the Cultural District is a 109-acre haven with 2,500 species of native and exotic plants in 29 specialty gardens. The Fort Worth Water Gardens adjacent to the Convention Center in downtown is a 2.3-acre urban oasis of fountains, cascades, and pools. It is scheduled to reopen in late 2006 following renovation.

On the western edge of the city, the Fort Worth Nature Center and Refuge, with more than 3,600 acres, is the largest city-owned nature center in the United States. It is a refuge for migratory birds and for animals, including a herd of buffalo, as well as for people, many of whom hike the 50 miles of trails. The setting also makes a great day trip for families.

For water-sports enthusiasts, the Fort Worth area has 18 lakes covering 100,000 acres for sailing, waterskiing, fishing, and pure enjoyment. They include Eagle Mountain Lake, home of the Fort Worth Boat Club, Lake Worth, Lake Grapevine, Lake Granbury, Lake Arlington, Benbrook Lake, and Joe Pool Lake. Kayakers can shoot down the Trinity River—or paddle, depending on the current.

Six Flags theme parks in nearby Arlington are other big attractions. At Six Flags Over Texas, a top draw for thrill seekers is the Titan, a roller coaster with one of the world's most dramatic drops. At Hurricane Harbor water park, visitors splash and swirl through the Tornado and other rides.

This page, top right: Kenny Perry is a two-time winner of the PGA Colonial tournament at the Colonial Country Club. Crowne Plaza now sponsors the event. This page, bottom left: The "Mean Green" University of North Texas football squad plays a home game at the campus in Denton. This page, bottom right: The Fort Worth Cats of the minors play at LaGrave Field. Opposite page: NASCAR drivers get the green flag at the Texas Motor Speedway.

Sports Town Extraordinaire

Fort Worth has sports for everyone. Major League Baseball fans can enjoy the Texas Rangers at nearby Arlington's Ameriquest Field, a state-of-the-art ballpark that harkens back to baseball temples like Wrigley Field and Fenway Park. The complex includes the Legends of the Game baseball museum. For professional football fans, the Dallas Cowboys will be playing at a new $650 million stadium in Arlington, scheduled to open in 2009. The 75,000-seat, retractable-roof stadium will be the new home for "America's Team".

For minor league baseball, LaGrave Field is the home of the Fort Worth Cats. The field provides stellar views of the downtown skyline as well as burgers grilled by local institution Kincaid's at its new ballpark location. Between 1926 and 1964, the ballpark fielded Hall of Famers including former Cats players Bobby Bragan, Duke Snider, Maury Wills, Sparky Anderson, Carl Erskine, and Rogers Hornsby.

Race fans can enjoy two NASCAR Nextel Cup races at the Texas Motor Speedway—the Samsung/RadioShack 500 in April and the Dickies 500 in November. The speedway is the country's second-largest sports and entertainment facility. Race weekends also feature Craftsman Truck and Busch Series action. Team Texas, the only stockcar driving school in the country that uses 2005 Nextel Cup cars and the current NASCAR Chevrolet SB2 racing engines, is based there.

The Professional Golfers Association (PGA) Tour makes an annual spring stop in Fort Worth for the Crowne Plaza Invitational at Colonial, sponsored by Crowne Plaza Hotels and Resorts beginning in 2007. The world's top golfers compete for a purse of more than $6 million and the coveted plaid jacket at historic Fort Worth Colonial Country Club. One of *Golf Magazine*'s top 100 courses, it is nicknamed "Hogan's Alley" for the five titles Ben Hogan won there. Other local clubs include Woodhaven, Shady Oaks, Ridglea, River Crest, Diamond Oaks, and Mira Vista.

Fort Worth Stock Show & Rodeo is considered one of the nation's top horse and livestock shows, drawing more than 950,000 attendees and entries from more than 40 states and many foreign countries. Highlights of the 109-year-old event, held in January and February, include the Stock Show Parade, the largest all-western parade in the world, and the "Bull's Night Out" Professional Rodeo Cowboys Association (PRCA) Extreme Bull Riding Event.

Lone Star Park at nearby Grand Prairie presents Thoroughbred racing, including the annual Lone Star Million, dubbed "the richest day in Texas horse racing," with six races cumulatively worth more than $1 million. The city

NATIONAL GUARD
INTERSTATE BATTERIES

catches Frog Fever when the Texas Christian University (TCU) Horned Frogs hit the gridiron at the 40,000-seat Amon G. Carter Stadium. Each year the Bell Helicopter Armed Forces Bowl matches top college football teams in a postseason battle televised by ESPN.

Hoops fans can enjoy TCU basketball played at the 7,200-seat Daniel-Meyer Coliseum. The Fort Worth Flyers, a team in the NBA Development League affiliated with the Dallas Mavericks, Philadelphia 76ers, and Charlotte Bobcats, play in the Fort Worth Convention Center, allowing fans to be right next to the action. The Dallas Mavericks, 2006 Western Conference NBA Champions, and the Dallas Stars professional hockey team play at American Airlines Center, designed by architect David M. Schwarz, who also designed Bass Hall and Ameriquest Field in Arlington.

Festivals

Fort Worth is famous for its festivals. In April, at the Main Street Arts Festival, tens of thousands of art lovers fill nine full blocks as artists and musicians from all over the country display their art. The four-day cultural event is ranked eighth nationally. At MayFest, children and adults can enjoy arts and entertainment on the banks of the Trinity River. Other annual events include ZestFest, hosted by Fort Worth–based *Chile Pepper* magazine; the Fort Worth Opera's four-week opera festival in the spring; the Alliance Air Show; the Red Steagall Cowboy Gathering and Western Swing Festival at the Stockyards; Jazz by the Boulevard in September; and the downtown Parade of Lights, where brightly lit floats ignite the holiday spirit.

Thriving Business Economy

Led by city officials and the business community, Fort Worth has nurtured a diverse economic environment that welcomes both major corporations and small start-ups. The city's thriving economy has grown beyond cattle and grain, railroads and airlines to include defense, technology, and oil and natural gas development.

USA Today and the nonprofit Partners for Livable Communities recently named Fort Worth and the surrounding region one of America's "Most Livable Large Cities." The Fort Worth Convention and Visitors Bureau effectively promotes the city's charms to vacationers, business travelers, and convention planners.

Companies appreciate the multiple benefits of Fort Worth. *Site Selection* magazine ranked Dallas–Fort Worth in the "Top Two

Opposite page: A bull rider hangs on during the Stockyards Championship Rodeo at the Cowtown Coliseum. This page, right: A Japanese festival is held at the Botanic Garden's Japanese Garden. This page, bottom left: A rodeo contestant and son enjoy a moment together.

Metropolitan Market" in securing new and expanded corporate facilities for the second year in a row in 2005. *Southern Business and Development* magazine in 2005 hailed it as the 2004 and 2005 "Mega Market of the Year." The magazine listed the region in its "Top 10 Headquarters Relocation Markets," citing its central location, superior air transportation, mild year-round climate, competitive operating and living costs, and its varied arts, sports, and entertainment scene.

The city is headquarters to a wide range of Fortune 500 and 1000 companies, including American Airlines, D. R. Horton, BNSF Railway, RadioShack, Pier 1 Imports, AmeriCredit, and XTO Energy. Located in the surrounding suburbs in Tarrant County are retailer GameStop, travel services firm Sabre Holdings, and insurance company HealthMarkets (formerly United Insurance Companies, Inc., or UICI). Other major corporate players include Lockheed Martin Aeronautics, Justin Brands, Williamson-Dickie, Acme Brick, and Ben E. Keith.

High-tech manufacturers include Nokia, Bell Helicopter, and Motorola, Inc. A growing center for biotech, Fort Worth has the University of North Texas (UNT) Health Science Center, the nearby University of Texas at Arlington (UTA) science and engineering programs, and corporations such as Alcon Laboratories, Galderma, and Healthpoint.

Fort Worth leadership has a tradition of reinvestment. Some two decades ago, the Bass family, including Sid Richardson Bass and his brothers Edward P., Lee M., and Robert, developed Sundance Square, a 20-block segment of historic downtown with brick-paved streets and tree-lined sidewalks that features a unique blend of offices, shops, restaurants, entertainment, and residential developments. In 2004, this cycle continued with both RadioShack and Pier 1 Imports investing more than $300 million to construct state-of-the-art headquarters downtown overlooking the Trinity River.

The city is business friendly, with state and local government providing a variety of incentives and support. Texas, a right-to-work state, offers refunds of state sales and use taxes on qualified expenditures for eligible businesses in designated state enterprise zones. The state allows local property-taxing

This page, top: New suburban homes in the Fort Worth area offer sunny spaces for growing families. This page, bottom left: Ryan Place is a historic neighborhood of stately homes, some nearly a century old. Opposite page, bottom right: The downtown renaissance is bringing popular new loft residences.

jurisdictions to partially or fully abate for up to 10 years a company's real and personal property taxes and, in other situations, sales taxes. In addition, freeport exemptions may apply for in-transit goods that leave the state within 175 days. Most locations in Fort Worth allow this exemption of school district, county, and city taxes, known as the "triple freeport" exemption.

Businesses can also take advantage of the city's Tax Increment Financing (TIF) reinvestment zones or Neighborhood Empowerment Zones, where owners may qualify for local property tax abatements or fee waivers on eligible expenses.

Large Labor Market

North Texas provides area companies with access to a labor force of more than three million. The rapidly growing population is projected to top seven million in the next 20 years. Area colleges produce about 30,000 graduates each year. About 70 percent of the region's population is white, with about 20 percent Hispanic (of any race) and approximately 13 percent black. Fort Worth's unemployment rate hovered at 5 percent during 2006.

Job training funds are available through a variety of programs, including the Texas' Skills Development Fund, which grants up to $500,000 for a single business for worker training. Fort Worth Works helps match job demands of the city with the community by coordinating job fairs year round.

A Great Place for Family, Friends, and Career

Fort Worth is one of the most affordable major cities in the country, with a cost-of-living index of 88.1 (100 is the national average). Housing costs are low, with an index of 77.3; grocery costs are below average, with an index of 90.8; and utility costs are below average at 92.2.

Home prices are one of the best things about Fort Worth. The average sale price for a single-family home in Fort Worth is $116,000, roughly half the national average of $227,533, and far below major Texas cities such as Austin ($173,100), Dallas ($162,600), and Houston ($151,000), according to the Texas Real Estate Center.

The area's diverse housing options include historic homes in century-old neighborhoods such as Ryan Place and Mistletoe Heights, charming bungalows in Fairmont and Arlington Heights, and new homes in planned communities such as Walsh Ranch. In the bustling suburbs of Southlake, Grapevine, Colleyville, and Keller, multimillion-dollar ranches sit side by side with country clubs and designer boutiques.

Redevelopment is also bringing new housing. In the Trinity River area, a $435 million revitalization is designed to transform the area north of downtown into a bustling hub of business and education. The Trinity River Vision project will also open up access to the river and enhance its natural ecosystems. Once complete, the waterfront area will have more than 10,000 residential units, three million square feet of commercial and retail space, and new facilities for Tarrant County College's downtown campus.

Fort Worth is not only affordable but is also safe. Its low crime rate earned it *Money* magazine's ranking of ninth-safest American city with a population of more than 500,000.

AN PLACE
Place
Elizabeth

LOFTS FOR SALE

Opposite page: University of North Texas in Denton has some 33,000 students. This page, top; Tarrant County College is building its fifth campus. This page, bottom: The University of Texas at Arlington houses more than 50 research centers and institutes.

Educational Opportunities Abound

Nationally recognized schools and universities give Fort Worth an unlimited potential for educational opportunities. Of the 21 independent school districts in Tarrant County, the largest is the Fort Worth Independent School District (FWISD), with more than 79,000 students. Its special programs include Montessori-based primary and specialty high school programs in math and science. The Council of the Great City Schools, Beating the Odds II, in a national study, cited FWISD as exemplary in narrowing learning gaps among racial groups in math and reading at all grade levels.

For higher education, the choices are many. The University of North Texas (UNT) flagship campus in nearby Denton, with more than 32,000 students, confers a wide range of degrees. A doctoral/research university, UNT ranks in the top four percent of U.S. colleges and universities classified by the Carnegie Foundation. UNT's Health Science Center is in Fort Worth. For the fifth year in a row, *U.S. News and World Report* ranked the school's Texas College of Osteopathic Medicine among the nation's top 50 medical schools for primary care.

Texas Christian University (TCU), with nearly 100 undergraduate majors, has been recognized by *Entrepreneur* magazine as one of the nation's "Top 100 Entrepreneurial Colleges and Universities". The *Wall Street Journal* has named TCU the top business school in Texas. *BusinessWeek* has recognized the university's undergraduate business program as one of the top 50 in the nation.

Texas Wesleyan University (TWU) has more than 2,700 students, with graduate programs in business, education, and nursing, as well as a law school. Construction has begun on a $2 million science and technology center.

Tarrant County College (TCC) offers associate's degrees, continuing education classes, and workforce development programs in business, health professions, computer science, and information technology. TCC has an enrollment of more than 34,000 at its four campuses throughout the county. A new 400,000-square-foot downtown campus is scheduled to open in 2008 with a skyway spanning the Trinity River.

For businesses and employees, Fort Worth is a great place to call home. Besides a strong economy, it has first-class dining, shopping, entertainment, and arts in a relaxed atmosphere that welcomes both business suits and blue jeans.

PART TWO
CHAMPIONS OF COMMERCE: FORT WORTH BUSINESS AND INDUSTRY

Opposite page: U.S. Air Force Chief of Staff General T. Michael Moseley speaks at the inauguration ceremony for the F-35 Lightning II joint strike fighter in Fort Worth. Lockheed Martin Aeronautics Company is developing the cutting-edge fighter. This page, bottom: Oil and gas are key drivers of the Fort Worth economy.

STRATEGIC RESOURCES

Aerospace and Energy

From its Cowtown roots to today's more diversified economy, Fort Worth has never left the staples behind. Crucial economic roles are still played by two strategic American resources with long histories in Fort Worth: a large aerospace and defense industry as well as ongoing contributions to U.S. and worldwide energy production now headlined by a local natural gas drilling boom.

Despite some rough patches, aerospace-defense has been a mainstay of the four-county Fort Worth–Arlington Metropolitan Division economy for more than 60 years. Aerospace-defense is Tarrant County's leading source of manufacturing employment, accounting for about one in four factory jobs in 2005. The ratio is almost that high across the four-county Fort Worth–Arlington Metropolitan Division.

Fort Worth also became a major player in the energy sector after oil was discovered about 100 miles west of here in 1917. Today, the Fort Worth area continues to attract oil-patch wildcatters and developers—and now, gas-patch explorers and producers, too.

Soaring to New Heights

The aerospace-defense industry was a logical outgrowth here as World War I brought U.S. Army Air Force aviation training. The 1920s gave birth to Braniff Airways and American Airlines flights serving the Fort Worth–Dallas area. World War II led to both aircraft manufacturing and a U.S. Air Force base. For the war effort, Consolidated Vultee Aircraft chose Fort Worth for a bomber factory, later acquired by General Dynamics, which shifted the plant to producing fighter jets. In 1993 the plant and aircraft operations were acquired by Lockheed Martin.

At a site next to the bomber factory, the Tarrant Field Airdrome of 1941 became Fort Worth Army Air Field in 1942. It was renamed Carswell Air Force Base in 1948, and became an early Strategic Air Command base, home to B-36 and later B-52 bombers.

In 1993, Carswell was closed under federal mandate and then reincarnated later in 1993 and 1994 as the home for the 301st Fighter Wing, the Naval Air Station Dallas military units and aircraft, and other similar military units and related operations. Today, the renamed Naval Air Station/Joint Reserve Base Fort Worth remains a major U.S. defense installation with about 1,500 personnel in 2006.

A major industry player in the region, Fort Worth–headquartered Lockheed Martin Aeronautics Company brought approximately $424 million to the region in 2005 through supply and service purchasing. For more than three decades, the company's Fort Worth operations (including the former General Dynamics Fort Worth Division) have developed, built, and marketed the F-16 Fighting Falcon, a military jet now used in 24 nations. In April 2006 Lockheed Martin celebrated delivering the 4,300th F-16. Part of Lockheed Martin of Bethesda, Maryland, the Fort Worth–based branch is involved in F-22 Raptor and F-35 Lightning II joint strike fighter development and production. The company is Tarrant County's second-largest employer.

The Fort Worth area's Bell Helicopter is a top 10 employer in Tarrant County, serving both the aerospace and defense sectors. A subsidiary of Providence, Rhode Island–based Textron, Bell expects to double its operating capacity to meet demand for the company's military and civilian helicopters, tilt-rotor aircraft, unmanned aircraft, and related products. Bell produces the V-22 Osprey tilt-rotor hybrid airplane/helicopter, the upgraded Marine Corps' H-1 Cobra, the JetRanger models, and a long lineup of other Bell helicopters. From 2004 to 2005, revenues for the Fort Worth–based subsidiary grew 29 percent, to a record $2.1 billion.

Many area companies grew as subcontractors and suppliers of Bell, Lockheed Martin, and other aerospace-defense giants. One of those is EFW, a Fort Worth–based branch of parent company Elbit Systems, based in Israel. EFW manufactures electronic systems and components for military aircraft, weapons, vehicles, naval vessels, and other equipment for U.S. armed forces and homeland security as well as similar uses by U.S. allies. EFW's products have gone into the F-16, F-35 JSF, Apache Attack helicopters, the V-22 Osprey, and rocket launchers, among other products, for clientele such as Boeing, Bell, and Lockheed Martin.

Opposite page: Fort Worth's 457th Fighter Squadron of the Air Force Reserve provides high-tech homeland defense while always ready for overseas deployment . Shown is the tail of the F-16 Fighting Falcon from Fort Worth's Lockheed Martin Aeronautics. Center: The FA-22 Raptor, the fifth-generation stealth fighter, is manufactured in part at Lockheed Martin Aeronautics. This page, bottom: Bell Helicopter's V-22 Osprey, a hybrid airplane/helicopter, flies faster, farther, and higher than conventional helicopters.

This page, top: This oil well pumps the "black gold" of Texas. This page, bottom: XTO Energy of Fort Worth is an oil-and-gas giant. Opposite page, top: Electricity hums across north Texas. Opposite page, bottom: This natural gas plant is part of the Barnett Shale boom that made the Fort Worth area the highest-volume gas-producing field in Texas.

'Barnett Play' Bonanza

Evidence of a surge in natural gas drilling abounds in the Fort Worth region, with wells dotting the urban landscape. Decades ago, wooden derrick "forests" dotted several east and west Texas landscapes; the present boom features sleek steel drilling rigs sprouting singly and in occasional clusters.

Roughnecks use new and improving high-tech methods to tap the bountiful natural gas locked in the Barnett Shale, a thick, mile-deep formation sprawling beneath prairies, farms, urban homes, skyscrapers, and under a dozen or more area counties. Known as "the Barnett Play" since the late 1990s, successful drilling into the Barnett Shale has made the Fort Worth region the highest-volume gas-producing field in Texas. Tarrant County ranks as one of the state's 10 top gas-producing counties, with wells pumping 94 billion cubic feet in 2005.

Soaring oil prices also have spurred a new rush in "black gold" production efforts. The industry is drilling new oil wells and reviving old ones across Texas and other states. That revival is attracting new businesses and retaining veteran companies in the Fort Worth region. Industry giant Halliburton Energy Services, a Houston-based oil and gas field services company, has deep roots with major area facilities.

Fort Worth's long ties with the petroleum industry remain strong, featuring many locally based energy explorers and producers. Fort Worth–based XTO Energy leases, owns, and operates oil and gas properties primarily in 10 states. In 2005 XTO Energy was the number-two natural gas producer and number-nine oil producer statewide. Also in 2005, XTO moved from the number-three to number-two Barnett Shale gas producer, pumping 56 billion cubic feet annually after acquiring a competitor's wells, according to *Fort Worth Star-Telegram* rankings, based on data from the state regulatory agency.

In 2005 *Star-Telegram* rankings limited to locally based companies, Bass Enterprises Production Company was the number-two Texas gas producer and number-four Texas oil producer. The company is held by the Bass family, including brothers Sid, Robert, Ed, and Lee Bass. The firm was developed by their late father, Perry Richardson Bass, and his uncle, famed wildcatter Sid W. Richardson.

The same *Star-Telegram* rankings named Range Resources/Range Production Company as number two in Texas oil and number three in Texas gas production. It may have boosted its local standings in 2006 by acquiring Fort Worth–based Stroud Energy's Barnett Shale production wells and other gas and oil properties.

Encore Operating/Encore Acquisition and Quicksilver Resources are among other leading locally based oil and gas producers.

Reaping the Benefits

Several Tarrant County–based companies have reaped benefits from increases in oil and Barnett Shale gas production. A stronghold in the petroleum-based products industry since 1933, Southwestern Petroleum of Fort Worth is a global company that produces and markets building maintenance and construction supplies and industrial lubricant oils, greases, and other oil-derived products. The company's petroleum-based wares are used in roofing, walls, flooring, pavement, metal structures, and other building components and in machinery lubrication. Subsidiary operations are in Belgium and Canada.

Providing support for oil and production companies, Harbison-Fischer Manufacturing Company is a major North American manufacturer of oil-field pumps, valves, tubing, rods, and related drilling and production parts and supplies. The company is based in nearby Crowley.

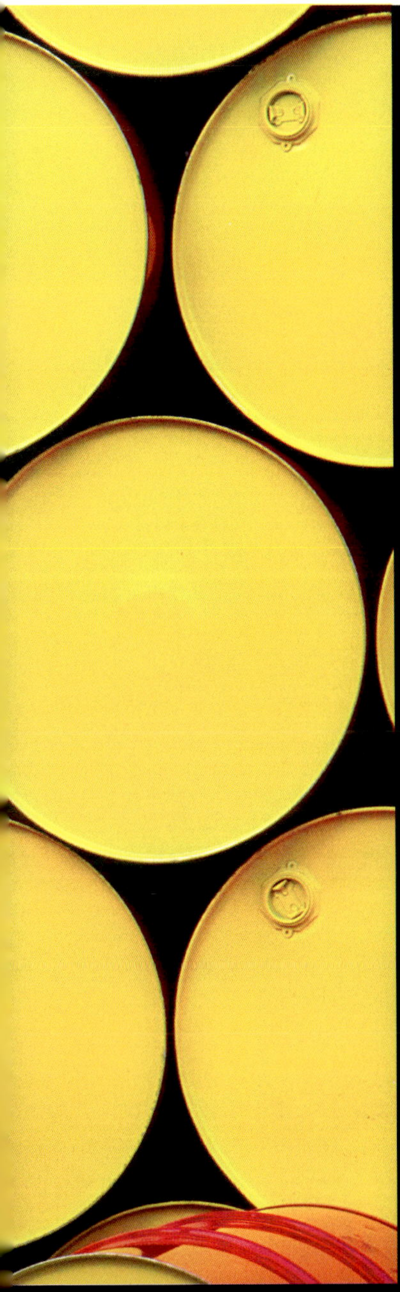

Opposite page: Peak prices per barrel brought a renewed investment in oil exploration and production in Texas. This page, bottom: Southwestern Petroleum of Fort Worth is a top manufacturer of petroleum-based products including engine oils, lubricants, and roof and floor coatings.

Another prominent global supplier is SPM Flow Control in west Fort Worth. The company provides oil and gas pumps, valves, mud pumps, flow-control and high-pressure transmission safety devices, and related equipment to the petroleum industry. It also offers field maintenance, repair, testing, and other oil and gas patch services.

When oil or other gas drilling prospects are being evaluated, industry players and landowners often turn to Fort Worth–based Cawley, Gillespie & Associates. Since 1961, the company has provided independent petroleum engineering services and geological evaluations for clients ranging from major oil conglomerates to property owners in North America and the United Kingdom.

Legendary wildcatters Sid W. Richardson and Perry R. Bass passed their company, Sid Richardson Carbon and Energy, to the Bass family. The company operates carbon-black plants in West Texas, the Texas Panhandle, and Louisiana and a West Texas electric power plant fueled by the carbon-black plant in Big Spring.

Many other oil and gas industry operators as well as major utilities also have home or branch offices in the Fort Worth and Dallas areas. For instance, Dallas-based TXU has roots in Fort Worth, Dallas, and the region dating to the 1880s and continues to be the dominant regional supplier of electric power.

Fort Worth area resources will continue to entice energy-focused businesses and the aerospace-defense industry.

Opposite page: More than 188,000 students attend Greater Fort Worth colleges and universities, which range from two-year institutions to graduate schools. This page: Much of Fort Worth's health care is centered in its Medical District, where hospitals such as Cook Children's Medical Center and Harris Methodist Fort Worth Hospital are located.

MIND AND BODY

Education and Health Care

Greater Fort Worth's esteemed educational and health care institutions nurture the mind and body. Approximately 140,000 workers contribute directly to Tarrant County's diverse education and health services via resources ranging from nationally ranked universities that attract many of the world's best minds to state-of-the-art medical centers and research facilities that cure maladies and save lives. Together, the area's educational and health care systems accommodate a rising demand for services accelerated by soaring population growth.

A Legacy of Learning

The Fort Worth area's institutions of higher education offer some of the best programs in the nation. In 2006 *U.S. News & World Report* ranked Texas Christian University (TCU) among the country's top 100 universities. TCU offers degree programs in education, science, technology, and ranch management, among others. Its M. J. Neeley School of Business has received academic accolades from *The Wall Street Journal*, *The Princeton Review*, and *BusinessWeek*. The Schieffer School of Journalism offers diverse programs including broadcast journalism, international communication, and public relation/advertising. The TCU Institute of Behavioral Research is a U.S. leader in drug-related research and a consultant on federal drug policy. In fall 2005, 8,749 students were enrolled at TCU, a record high that included 7,171 undergraduates majoring in 97 programs. The 1,578 students in graduate and professional programs pursued degrees in 60 programs.

Another noted Fort Worth institution is Texas Wesleyan University. In 2005 the school enrolled 2,700 U.S. and international students in traditional academics as well as evening and weekend classes for nontraditional, commuter students. The university is well known for its programs, including undergraduate liberal arts and sciences, nursing, and graduate education and law. Located downtown, Texas Wesleyan School of Law is fully accredited by the American Bar Association. Law school graduates have performed admirably on the annual bar exam with an 82.5 percent passing rate in 2006. That same year, 42 alumni were sworn into the U.S. Supreme Court Bar.

Opposite page, top: Programs at Southwestern Baptist Theological Seminary range from preparing students for ministries and missions to training them to become church musicians. Opposite page, bottom: The University of Texas at Arlington's nanotechnology laboratory is the site of research into electrolytic plasma processing, among many other areas. This page, top: Engineering is one of many subjects taught at local colleges. This page, bottom: The prestigious M. J. Neeley School of Business at Texas Christian University was ranked the top business school in Texas by *The Wall Street Journal* in 2006.

Students also come from across the globe to attend Fort Worth's Southwestern Baptist Theological Seminary. The second-largest nationally accredited U.S. seminary, Southwestern Baptist had 3,535 students in fall 2005 who were pursuing diploma, bachelor's, master's, doctoral, or research degrees in theology and philosophy, Christian evangelism and counseling, Christian music, pastoral studies, and other disciplines. Most of the students who have graduated since the school's founding in 1908 have earned graduate degrees.

The largest university in Tarrant County is the University of Texas at Arlington (UTA), which enrolled 25,352 students from 150 nations in fall 2005. UTA excels in myriad disciplines and programs, from training engineers, artists, criminologists, and teachers to exploring cutting-edge electronics to researching urban growth and social issues. In spring 2006 UTA was ranked fourth in state research grants, receiving more than $733,000, the largest sum awarded to a school in the North Texas region. Some of UTA's state-of-the-art research centers include the Nanotechnology Research and Training Facility, one of a few such facilities nationwide that focus on building micro devices, and the Automation and Robotics Research Institute, estimated to have a $770 million, 15-year regional economic impact with new inventions, patents, and technology upgrades. Like most other regional universities, UTA is friendly to both commuters and campus residents, exemplifying the diversity of academic experiences.

With 12 residence halls, the University of North Texas in Denton is the largest regional school with students living on campus. With 32,000 students, the public university has received recognition for its academics, low tuition, and amenities. Also in Denton, Texas Woman's University is the country's largest university geared toward women.

Fort Worth–Arlington offers quality education to students attending two-year colleges, job-training programs, and other schools. The largest of these schools is Tarrant County College (TCC), with four area campuses plus one being built downtown. Since 1998 TCC has documented increasing enrollment; in fall 2005, the college had 34,403 students pursuing associate's degrees and certificate programs through a range of arts and sciences, job-training programs, and other curricula. Additionally, the college offers specialized programs, such as one for academically advanced high school students. The first phase of the fifth campus is expected to open in 2008.

Opposite page: Heath care and education combine at Fort Worth hospitals. This page, above: Tarrant County's health care industry employs more than 80,000 people. This page, below: The University of North Texas Health Science Center at Fort Worth is home to the only school of osteopathic medicine in Texas.

A Healthy Outlook

Growing with the demands of an ongoing population influx, Fort Worth–Arlington's health care industry includes more than 80,000 employees in Tarrant County who work at respected medical centers and institutions. One of those is the highly regarded University of North Texas Health Science Center at Fort Worth, which was rated by *U.S. News & World Report* in 2006 as one of the nation's top 50 medical schools for primary care medicine. The center emphasizes training students for a rural medical practice, and students perform their primary care residency in family and internal medicine at Plaza Medical Center of Fort Worth, while other graduate programs are conducted at Fort Worth's John Peter Smith Hospital.

More than 1,000 students in Fort Worth are training at the center's Texas College of Osteopathic Medicine, School of Public Health, and Graduate School of Biomedical Sciences. UNT Health Science Center researchers are studying a wide range of maladies such as diabetes, cancer, Alzheimer's, and heart disease, as well as biomedical sciences such as pharmacology, neuroscience, molecular biology, and immunology. Annual research funding has exceeded $20 million for two consecutive school years through 2005–06. A large share came from the National Institutes of Health.

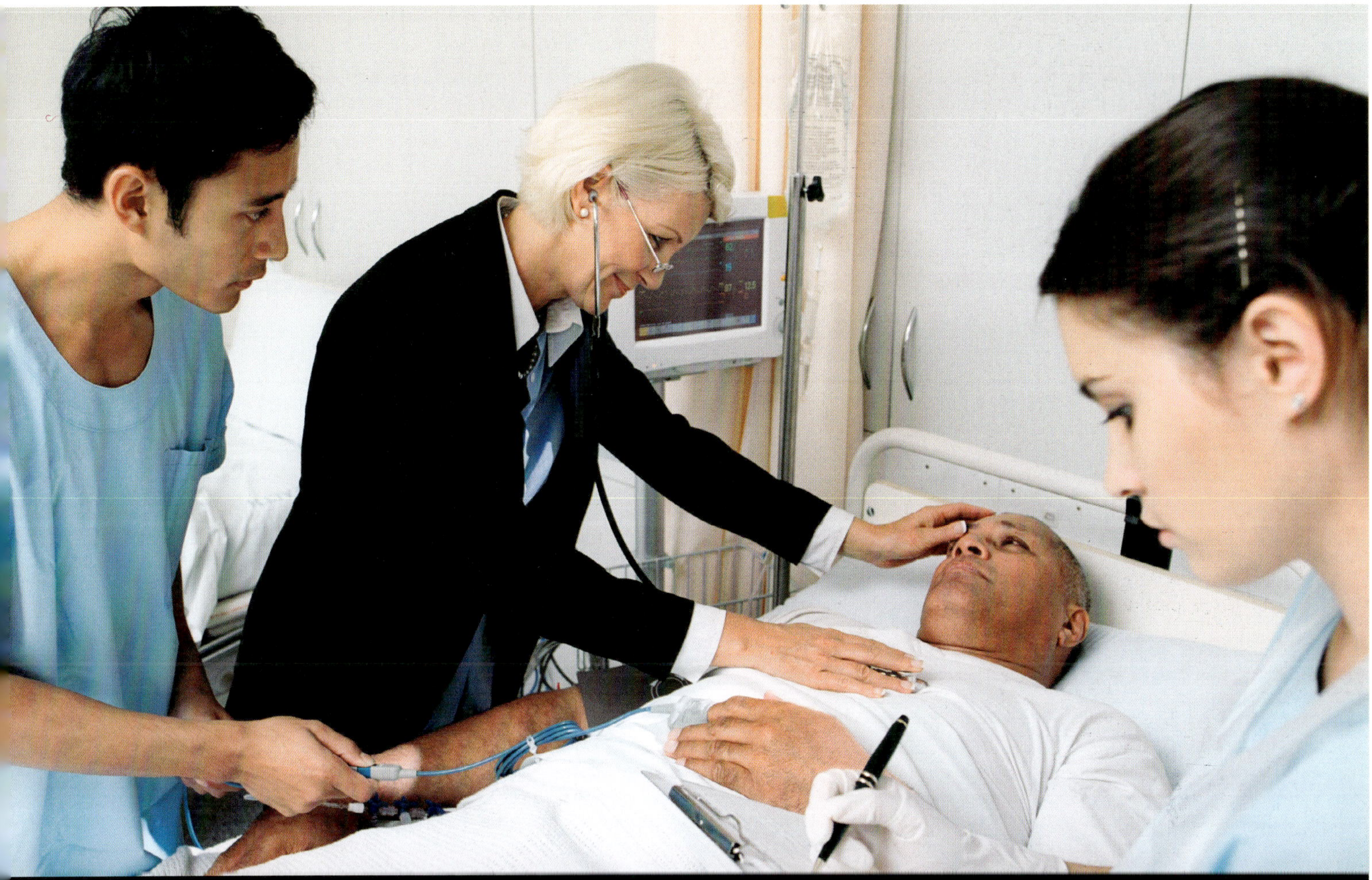

The center's researchers collaborate with many North Texas hospitals, including Baylor All Saints Medical Center at Fort Worth, Baylor All Saints Medical Center at Southwest Fort Worth, and Baylor Regional Medical Center at Grapevine. The hospitals, which employ approximately 1,780 people in Tarrant County, are part of Dallas-based Baylor Health Care System.

Baylor All Saints Medical Center at Fort Worth is undergoing an estimated $129 million expansion that includes a stand-alone, 170,000-square-foot women's hospital that will specialize in reproductive and obstetrical medicine, gynecological surgery, genetic testing, and other services. It will provide a Level III intensive care unit for premature and low-birth-weight infants, a breast cancer center, and other facilities.

The medical community hub is the Fort Worth Medical District, just south of downtown. It features Texas Health Resources, one of Tarrant County's top six employers, with about 8,050 employees at Harris Methodist Fort Worth Hospital, Arlington Memorial Hospital, Harris Methodist H-E-B Hospital, Harris Methodist Northwest, Harris Methodist Southwest, and related facilities that stretch into the Fort Worth–Arlington–Dallas Metroplex.

Serving the area since 1930, Harris Methodist Fort Worth Hospital is the city's flagship medical facility and the largest in Tarrant County, with more than 800 staff physicians and 700 beds. Additionally, the medical campus has more than 4,000 employees and 200 volunteers. In May 2006 the American College of Surgeons redesignated Harris Methodist Fort Worth a Level II Adult Trauma Center.

Opening in phases in 2005 and 2006, near the flagship hospital, the high-tech $62 million Harris Methodist Heart Center is focused on providing state-of-the-art cardiovascular medicine. The center's services range from the latest digital imaging to locating blocked arteries to surgeries, complete implants, and diagnostics.

In 2006 Harris Methodist Southwest Hospital was doubling in size with a $60 million upgrade that included expanded services and additional beds, equipment, and staffing.

With its flagship hospital complex in Fort Worth, JPS Health Network employs approximately 3,300 people and is Tarrant County's tax-supported medical service, offering reduced-cost care for eligible patients at John Peter Smith Hospital, a certified Level II Trauma Center with an intensive care unit and an AIDS treatment center. JPS also has a $90 million, 100-bed patient tower under construction in Fort Worth, which will house surgical suites and diagnostic and trauma facilities.

Fort Worth–based Cook Children's Health Care System provides more than 30 pediatric services—from newborn intensive care to stem cell and bone marrow transplants—at its Cook Children's Medical Center and related facilities. Each year, about one million procedures, therapies, surgeries, and consultations are performed systemwide. To accommodate rising demand, Cook Children's Health Care System opened a $53 million addition in 2003, expanding its critical and patient care facilities. The system, whose patients come from around the world, has more than two dozen local branches and affiliations.

Opposite page: Forty cardiologists are on staff at the new, $62 million Harris Methodist Heart Center. The center is part of Arlington-based Texas Health Resources, a nonprofit health care system comprising 13 hospitals in North Texas. This page: One of the more than 500 physicians at Cook Children's Medical Center poses with a young patient. The hospital, whose roots date to 1918, has more than 200 beds.

Another major hospital complex is Huguley Memorial Medical Center in south Fort Worth. The facility includes an acute care hospital with more than 210 beds, a hospice care center, and approximately 300 primary care and specialty physicians.

Fort Worth has a wide range of medical services, from comprehensive care at Plaza Medical Center, to specialized diagnosis and treatment for all types of neurological problems at Neurological Services Texas, to anti-aging therapies at The Institute of Age Management and Aesthetic Medicine.

When it comes to critical health care or the education needed for today's competitive marketplace, Fort Worth–Arlington's institutions provide some of the nation's best.

Opposite page: From financial packages to office design, Fort Worth professional firms tailor their services to meet the needs of businesses large or small. This page, both photos: The metroplex's financiers range from international mutual fund company Fidelity Investments (top) to pawn lender Cash America International (bottom).

STELLAR SUPPORT

Finance, Insurance, and Professional Services

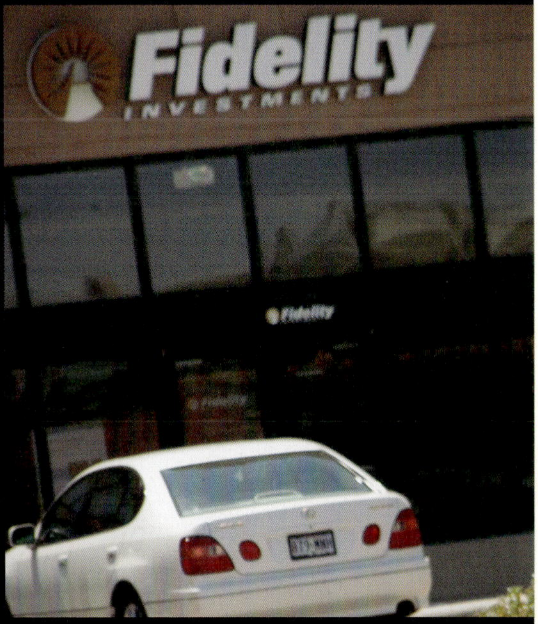

The Fort Worth region's robust economy and high quality of life owe much of their success to the financial and business services industries. The area boasts a financial industry attuned to the diverse metroplex business community. Fort Worth's insurance industry is diverse, too, providing plans tailored to individual and business needs, and its professional services sector thrives, from esteemed architectural and engineering firms to storied law and accounting offices.

Building Assets

Fort Worth's financial services sector is strong, with nearly 16,000 workers in 2005 employed at branch offices for global financial firms such as Chase Bank, Bank of America, and Fidelity Investments. Fort Worth is headquarters to major financial companies. For instance, Fort Worth–based Cash America International offers secured, nonrecourse loans to economically disenfranchised residents in 21 states, including Texas, at its 464 Cash America pawnshops. The diversified company also provides 286 cash-advance locations under the business names Cashland and Cash America Payday Advance, as well as approximately 140 Mr. Payroll check cashing centers. Altogether, Cash America International, the nation's first publicly owned pawn lender chain, loaned nearly $1.4 billion in pawn loans and cash advances in 2005. In 2006, the company expanded with an agreement to buy CashNetUSA, an online cash lender.

This page: State National Bancshares, the holding company for State National Bank, had $1.7 billion in total assets at the end of 2005. Opposite page, top: American Airlines Federal Credit Union, which has two branches in Fort Worth, has a total $4 billion in assets. Opposite page, bottom: San Francisco money giant Wells Fargo has five offices in Fort Worth and $500 billion in assets.

A more traditional financial institution, State National Bancshares in Fort Worth serves as the main subsidiary for holding company State National Bank, which provides basic banking services such as checking, savings, and money market accounts at more than 40 branches in 24 cities in Texas and New Mexico. State National also offers phone and online services, individual retirement accounts, and home loans. Real estate comprises more than half of its portfolio of loans, which includes personal, commercial, and agricultural. The financial firm is targeting Fort Worth for expansion efforts.

OmniAmerican Bank is another stalwart institution in Fort Worth. Established in 1956 as a credit union serving Carswell Air Force Base personnel, the firm offers a full-service menu from checking and savings accounts to mortgage loans. Formerly OmniAmerican Credit Union, the bank has 17 offices in the Fort Worth–Arlington–Dallas metroplex, with five in Fort Worth. In 2006 OmniAmerican served 158 communities and had nearly $1.5 billion in assets.

Other major banks in the area include Worthington National Bank, Citizens National Bank, and Compass Bank.

First Command Financial Services in Fort Worth also got its start in the 1950s—1958, to be exact—serving families at Carswell Air Force Base. Today, the company and its subsidiaries offer financial services to nearly 300,000 active and retired U.S. military members and their families. Products include trust and estate planning, insurance, mortgages and other loans, mutual fund investments, and banking basics such as checking and savings accounts.

Another stronghold in the Fort Worth financial sector is American Airlines Federal Credit Union, started in 1936 by employees of the transportation company. Membership today is open to all airline industry employees; in 2006, that included approximately 200,000 people. With branches in 20 U.S. cities and Puerto Rico, the Fort Worth–based credit union has a lending program to help members finance homes, cars, and education. It also sells credit life and credit disability insurance.

With approximately 2,000 workers, AmeriCredit is a major employer in Fort Worth's financial sector. The company is a top financier to more than one million vehicle-buying consumers in the United States and Canada. Headquartered in Fort Worth, the firm caters mainly to customers with credit limitations or problems by buying loans and, each month, funding an estimated 1,400 subprime loans—mostly for used vehicles—via a processing center in Arlington. The company also has offices in Arizona, North Carolina, and Canada. AmeriCredit's loan portfolio was approximately $12 billion in 2006.

Credit Unio

WELLS
FARGO
TOWER
DONT WALK
OPEN

Safeguarding the Future

From health to life insurance policies, the area's insurance sector aims to ensure that Fort Worth citizens are protected. HealthMarkets, based in North Richland Hills, and its subsidiaries operate in 44 states and provide health and life insurance to 1.2 million members who represent an underserved market in the insurance industry, primarily the self-employed, students, hourly workers, and small-business owners and their employees. Formerly UICI, it changed its name in 2006 to reflect its mission of providing consumers with affordable policies and innovative industry approaches. For example, the company invests in state-of-the-art technology so consumers can comparison shop for health care providers and hospitals. The company has 4,000 independent health insurance agents and 10,000 life insurance agents.

Fort Worth is home to American Health Underwriters, which provides medical coverage for the self-employed and for individuals and families. With more than 2,500 sales associates, the company nets more than $50 million of new business each year. Its plans are consumer friendly, with flexible payment options and a full-range of services.

Fort Worth is also home to the National Farm Life Insurance Company, the largest life insurance company headquartered in Texas that sells solely to the state's residents.

Nonstandard automobile insurance is the focus of Hallmark Financial Services, which also caters to people who might have trouble qualifying for comprehensive plans elsewhere. The Fort Worth–based company and its subsidiaries underwrite policies for drivers nationwide.

Opposite page: National Farm Life Insurance Company, housed in its landmark building on Fort Worth's east side, is the largest Texas insurance company with an exclusively Texan clientele. This page: Architects Carter & Burgess, in the Carter Burgess Plaza in Fort Worth, has a client list that includes CVS/pharmacy and American Airlines.

Getting Down to Business

The Fort Worth region offers some of the nation's finest professional services businesses. One of the best known and largest architectural and engineering firms nationwide is Fort Worth–based Carter & Burgess, with 32 offices in 19 states and more than six decades of consistent award-winning experience. With 3,000 employees and nearly $500 million in revenue in 2006, the firm is equipped to tackle projects as diverse as serving as the lead engineering and environmental impact consultant on the Southeast High Speed Rail Project to designing part of the Trinity Railway Express in downtown Fort Worth to completing studies for an air cargo center at Dallas/Fort Worth International Airport. From London to Los Angeles, Houston to Hawaii, Carter & Burgess imprints its talent on the world.

Headquartered in Fort Worth, Gideon Toal has left its mark, too. Besides architecture, the company serves the planning, economic development, interior design, structural engineering, and landscape architecture sectors. The half-century-old firm has received accolades for many of its projects, including five industry design awards for its work on a circuit board plant at Alliance Airport for France-based Valeo Electronics.

Based in Fort Worth, Freese and Nichols provides a range of architectural and engineering services, but specializes in water management projects. The firm helped to launch White Rock Lake, one of the state's first municipal water-supply reservoirs; it also offers input on water policy. The company has offices in five other Texas cities.

The civil engineering firm Dunaway Associates worked on the 21-story Pier 1 Imports headquarters and on Walsh Ranch, a master-planned community.

The Fort Worth area also is known for its other professional services, including respected law and accounting firms. Cantey & Hanger, a full-service civil law firm, is one of the oldest in the Southwest. Its 80 attorneys specialize in such areas as appellate, finance, and tax.

With 32 practice areas, Shannon, Gracey, Ratliff & Miller is a leading law firm in the Southwest. Many of its attorneys are frequently honored—such as in the August 2006 issue of *The American Lawyer*—for their work in areas such as commercial, corporate, and labor and employment law. With its home office in Fort Worth, the firm has five other locations in Texas, including Arlington and Dallas.

One of the largest law offices in the Fort Worth–Arlington–Dallas metroplex is Law, Snakard & Gambill. Based in Fort Worth, the full-service firm offers a wide array of expertise but specializes in practice areas such as health, litigation, and real estate.

Opposite page: Fort Worth claims numerous firms, Freese and Nichols and Dunaway Associates among them, that are capable of mounting large-scale civil engineering projects. This page: Well-respected Fort Worth law firms such as Jackson Walker LLP and Decker, Jones, McMackin, McClane, Hall & Bates stand ready to defend their clients' rights and interests.

Other renowned firms include Jackson Walker LLP and Decker, Jones, McMackin, McClane, Hall & Bates.

Fort Worth's accounting firms are equally impressive. McCaslin & Company, a full-service public accounting firm in Fort Worth, serves a diversity of clients from individuals to limited-liability companies to nonprofits in industries such as manufacturing, oil and gas, and insurance.

Also a full-service public accounting firm in Fort Worth, Sproles Woodard has offices in Texas and New Mexico. Its specialty practice areas include taxation and planning, audit and assurance, and management consulting. The firm serves approximately 1,700 individual and commercial clients.

The Fort Worth region's central location provides an economic boost to these sectors by attracting major employers and giving professionals a stage from which to parlay their services to the world.

Opposite page: The private firm of DFB Pharmaceuticals and its affiliates produce and market innovative pharmaceuticals and over-the-counter medicines. This page: Manufactured products in Fort Worth can be as familiar and homey as tortilla chips—which area producers ship across the world, from South America to North Africa.

WORKING FOR THE WORLD

Manufacturing and Food Processing

Metro Fort Worth–Arlington is a diverse manufacturing and food processing hub that generates products as varied as boots and bread, pharmaceuticals and pickles, and computer chips and tortilla chips. Approximately 2,200 manufacturing and food processing companies operate in the four-county metropolitan area, working, literally, for the world.

Fort Worth's factory trades evolved from the no-nonsense attitudes of the Old West. The same Trinity River that brought the cavalry here in 1849 also bred a commerce center first tied to cattle, mules, and horses. Then came the railroads, bringing beef, pork, lamb, and poultry packers; grain merchants; flour millers; feed makers; and cotton merchants. Oil-drilling wildcatters and military aircraft builders followed.

Thanks to industrial diversification, Fort Worth–area manufacturing and food-processing employment is a stubbornly steady and resilient sector. Through early 2006, metro-area factory employment on average increased from the year before by nearly 1,000 jobs in Tarrant, Johnson, Parker, and Wise counties. Factory employment in the Fort Worth region also outperformed that of many comparable U.S. markets.

Making It in Fort Worth

Manufacturing is a major economic engine. Metro Fort Worth–Arlington accounts for more than one in 10 manufacturing jobs statewide. Besides prominent locally based manufacturers, the Fort Worth region is home to many major plants for out-of-state companies such as Michigan-based General Motors, a top-25 Tarrant County employer with about 3,000 auto assembly workers.

Opposite page: Optical supplies manufacturer Alcon, producer of such familiar ophthalmic products as Opti-Free, makes its U.S. home in Fort Worth. This page, top: Galderma Laboratories, a joint venture of Nestlé and L'Oréal, specializes in skin care. This page, bottom: Coria Laboratories, an affiliate of DFB Pharmaceuticals and a division of Healthpoint, produces treatments for diseases of the skin, hair, and nails.

Part of the overall industry's success stems from the support it receives from Fort Worth–area groups. One is the Texas Manufacturing Assistance Center, a state-federal venture led by major Texas universities that has provided planning, training, and consulting services to boost the competitiveness of more than 3,000 Texas manufacturers. Another aid is the University of Texas at Arlington's Automation and Robotics Research Institute, which has worked with 3,000-plus companies to upgrade manufacturing efficiencies.

Medical manufacturing is a robust niche in the region. Alcon, headquartered in Fort Worth, began in 1945 as a small pharmacy and has grown into one of Tarrant County's four largest manufacturing employers. Majority-owned by Switzerland-based Nestlé, S.A., Alcon is a world-leading maker of eye-treatment pharmaceuticals, related eye-care products, and eye-surgery equipment. It serves clientele in more than 180 countries. With worldwide facilities and more than 13,000 employees systemwide, the company maintains its headquarters and two major plants in Fort Worth. Alcon employs approximately 3,000 at its headquarters.

Another medical manufacturer with global impact is Fort Worth–based DFB Pharmaceuticals, which makes medicines for skin and tissue management, medical devices, and over-the-counter drugs. Privately held DFB has more than 250 employees locally and 1,800 worldwide. Its divisions and related companies include Healthpoint, Ltd. and Coria Laboratories, Ltd.

Other major Fort Worth manufacturers in the medical field include Galderma Laboratories, a global pharmaceutical maker focused on dermatology, and international giant Medtronic, which produces medical technology and products. Based in Europe, Galderma employs 150 at its U.S. home in Fort Worth. Medtronic, headquartered in Minneapolis, relies on approximately 210 Fort Worth employees to make instruments for use in cardiovascular, neurological, and other surgeries.

Alcon
OPTI-FREE
Express

Opposite page: In the business since 1891, Acme Brick is the official brick maker for five major league sports franchises, including the Dallas Cowboys. This page, both photos: The Williamson-Dickie Manufacturing Company (top) on West Vickery Boulevard makes the superdurable Dickies line of work clothes, while Justin Brands (bottom) on West Dagget Avenue is famous for its western boots.

Local manufacturing includes the high-tech sector with Fort Worth's TTI, one of the world's leading suppliers of electronic connectors and related circuit board components. The privately held company, which serves clientele in Europe, Asia, and the Americas, has 34 branches in the United States as well as 26 international offices. It also operates Mouser Electronics, an electronics distribution subsidiary in nearby Mansfield.

Fort Worth's high-tech manufacturing niche extends to National Semiconductor in Arlington. The computer chip maker has a portfolio of more than 3,000 products, primarily for analog and mixed-signal uses. The electronic parts go into office automation systems, personal computers, communications equipment, automotive parts, and other industrial and consumer applications across North America.

On the electronics finished-product end, Uniden America Corporation in Fort Worth is the U.S. subsidiary of the Japan company Uniden, which produces, among other devices, cordless telephones, telecommunications systems, and networking and data products. Fort Worth–based staff members sell Uniden products through dealers and distributors in North, Central, and South America.

Boots and Bricks

Metro Fort Worth's influence in the apparel industry is significant. From durable work wear to cowboy boots, U.S. presidents and celebrities sport Fort Worth's finest threads. Williamson-Dickie Manufacturing Company debuted in Fort Worth in 1922 as a local bib-overall cutting and sewing operation. Today, the company is the world's largest work wear producer, with Dickies brand of khaki, denim, flannel shirts, pants, jeans, overalls, jackets, and other lines noted for consistent durability and comfort. Such attributes have made Dickies popular with Americans of all walks of life, from oilmen to pop singers to NASCAR racers. The brand is sold in more than 60 countries.

Boot-maker Justin Brands is another renowned global brand with Fort Worth roots. Formed in 1879 to repair the boots of cowboys driving longhorns up the Chisholm Trail, Justin established headquarters in Fort Worth in 1925. Expansion ensued when the company become Justin Industries in 1968. It spent the succeeding decades acquiring competitors such as Nocona Boot, Chippewa Shoes, and Tony Lama Boots; during the 1980s, the company became the world's largest boot maker, a title it has since maintained. In 2000 Berkshire Hathaway, famed billionaire Warren E. Buffett's company in Omaha, Nebraska, bought Justin Industries for $600 million. Justin Brands is a major contributor to Berkshire Hathaway's multibillion-dollar apparel group.

Justin Boots wasn't the only attraction for Berkshire Hathaway. Justin Industries also includes Fort Worth–based Acme Brick, another dominant U.S. brand that helped to contribute to Justin Industries' overall success. Located in Fort Worth since 1911, Acme Brick is the nation's largest brick maker, operating 23 plants with annual output capacity exceeding one billion bricks and employing 2,960 workers, including approximately 240 in the Fort Worth area.

Acme Brick is just one example of metro Fort Worth's construction manufacturing subsector. Chemical Lime is another. The company is the U.S. headquarters for Belgium-based Lhoist Group, Europe's leading lime producer. Chemical Lime, which operates more than 50 sites in 20 states plus ventures in Mexico and Canada, extracts lime through its kilns and delivers lime and lime-based products to customers in construction, chemical, steel, metal, mining, pulp-paper, municipal public works, and environmental improvement trades.

Fort Worth's Quorum International is a construction supplier of a different genre. The company is a leading manufacturer of ceiling fans, chandeliers, pendants, and other light fixtures and has distributed millions of its products to builders and homeowners.

American Metal Services of Fort Worth is a metal distributor, providing hard-to-find metals for specialty markets. For used metal and other materials, Gamtex Industries is one of Fort Worth's largest recyclers. It has been in business since 1913.

Helping Fort Worth's varied industries get production going and keep it going is DFW Movers and Erectors, which moves machinery and installs industrial equipment. DFW is one of the leading rigging and millwright contractors in the nation.

Cowtown Bred "Chowtown"

Fort Worth in the Old West served as a convenient stop for hungry and thirsty cowboys. It also attracted cattle traders, flour millers, feed makers, and other food-processing companies, including both locally based businesses and, much later, facilities owned by well-known businesses such as the Dannon Company and Miller Brewing. Today, the food industry is so pervasive that the *Fort Worth Star-Telegram* in 1998 dubbed the area "Chowtown."

Deliciously fresh bread, pies, and cakes launched Mrs Baird's Bakeries in 1908. Started in a kitchen by a woman who baked to support her ailing husband and eight children, the company became a Texas institution that at one time operated 10 commercial bakeries. Grupo Bimbo, a Mexican baking conglomerate, bought the company in 1998. Today, Mrs Baird's operates under the Bimbo Bakeries USA banner, with Fort Worth serving as U.S. headquarters. Its products, distributed nationwide, include brands such as Oroweat, Tia Rosa, Marinela, Francisco, Bimbo, and Mrs Baird's.

Opposite page: O. B. Macaroni Company has been making Texas-size noodles for four generations. This page: Other Fort Worth foodstuff makers include Best Maid, noted for its pickles (top) and relishes, and Leo's Foods (bottom), producer of tortillas, chips, and taco shells.

Dalton's Best Maid Products established its mouthwatering reputation in the 1920s with homemade condiments such as mayonnaise, sandwich spread, and relish sold at a family-operated grocery store. Today, the Fort Worth company's marketing area includes 15 states. Known primarily for its pickles, Best Maid produces edibles for grocery and food-service customers that include restaurants and Wal-Mart. The company operates its own cucumber-processing farm in nearby Mansfield and a pickle and condiment processing plant in Fort Worth.

Always loving its South-of-the-Border heritage, Fort Worth has generated many Mexican food makers, including Leo's Foods. Leo's was founded in 1978 with four employees who produced tortillas and chips for neighbors and restaurants. The company built a modern factory in 1993 and continued to expand. In 2006 approximately 275 employees produced corn, flour, and flavored tortillas, nacho chips, and taco shells for more than 100 grocery, food-service, and private-label customers in 28 states, Brazil, and Egypt.

Metro Fort Worth's diversity in the food industry is exemplified once again—this time with pasta. Founded as the Fort Worth Macaroni Company in 1899 and renamed for its brand in 1959, O. B. "Our Best" Macaroni Company is family owned and operated. Each year it produces 10 million pounds of pasta, in all shapes and varieties, at its Fort Worth plant.

Like the Texas frontier that gave birth to Fort Worth's manufacturing and food processing companies, the industries today are wide open for continued success.

RAVE
MOTION PICTURES
[the future now showing

Opposite page: Northeast Mall, one of the largest malls in the Southwest, features five anchors and 140 specialty shops as well as Rave Motion Pictures. This page: An award-winning model of urban redevelopment, Sundance Square is regarded as one of the most exciting and pedestrian-friendly downtown areas in this country.

A PEOPLE PLACE

Real Estate, Construction, and Development

Fort Worth is a pioneer in urban renaissance. The area's revival surged during the 1980s and 1990s, when approximately 20 blocks of a shopping, commercial, office, entertainment, and residential district known as Sundance Square resuscitated development across downtown Fort Worth. The past quarter century also witnessed renovated regional malls, upgrades, and restoration in the area's Cultural, Stockyards, and Medical districts.

The Texas Motor Speedway in Fort Worth added more zest to the area's ongoing economic expansion, as did the Alliance Texas project, a master-planned public-private development that includes the world's first industrial-driven airport as well as commercial and office sites, residential neighborhoods, a sculpted golf course, and open ranch land with roaming buffalo and cattle. Aided by a cargo transportation–industrial park hub along Interstate 35W, Alliance Texas's economic impact on the north Texas region is estimated at more than $26 billion since its inception in the late 1980s.

Today, redevelopment and new growth continue to accelerate in Fort Worth and Tarrant County. Throughout the four-county Fort Worth–Arlington metropolitan area, the number of new residential subdivisions, superstores, shopping centers, and Main Street rebirths continue to grow. Other amenities also are coming. Already home to Major League Baseball's Texas Rangers, the City of Arlington will welcome the National Football League's Dallas Cowboys to a new stadium for the 2009 season. The team will move from Irving in adjacent Dallas County.

Jewel on the Trinity

Downtown Fort Worth is poised for another renaissance. Its Trinity River Vision (TRV) development project promises to forge Cowtown charm into an inner city jewel on a restructured, beautified Trinity River, a waterway that brought the U.S. Cavalry, which built a fort here in 1849, and, for more than a century, loomed as a severe flood threat. In 2005 and 2006 the river's future potential surfaced with the projected $435 million Trinity Uptown project; the first TRV phase calls for a 1.5-mile-long bypass river channel, new dams, a lake, a major river pollution cleanup, and an extensive city drainage upgrade to replace the decades-old levee system. Site work began in 2006.

Trinity Uptown's future 33-acre recreational lake, two islands, bridges, and levee-cleared river and lake fronts are forecast to generate development on downtown's north-northwestern perimeter and to revive the economically challenged area between Fort Worth's thriving downtown and the northside tourist magnet Stockyards National Historic District. Condominiums, apartments, restaurants, shops, offices, parks, tree-lined walkways, biking trails, and other amenities are expected to sprout along Trinity Uptown's shores and adjacent areas.

In fact, TRV's mixed-use economic development concept is already materializing, with two staff-nurturing corporate campuses on the downtown river bank. In 2004 Fort Worth–headquartered Pier 1 Imports, a global chain of furniture and home décor stores, moved into its modern 20-story, $100 million glass, metal, and gray granite headquarters beside the river. The tower has 460,000 square feet and houses about 800 Pier 1 employees. In 2004 and 2005 Fort Worth–based RadioShack Corporation, an electronics retail chain, moved more than 2,000 employees into its sleek and spacious glass, brick, and limestone headquarters on its 37-acre "Riverfront Campus." The $227 million, 900,000-square-foot complex is Pier 1's neighbor.

Opposite page: Trinity Uptown is a bold waterfront development plan to revitalize an 800-acre area north of downtown and create an exciting area to live, work, and play. This page, right: Once slated to be demolished, The Tower (formerly the Bank One Tower) was refurbished, expanded, and reopened in 2005. This page, left: The goal of the Trinity River Vision is to preserve and enhance some 88 miles of the river and its tributaries, while promoting a healthy, vibrant downtown and preventing urban sprawl.

An Urban Rebirth

Downtown Fort Worth's residential rebirth started with Sundance Square. However, when a deadly tornado struck the city's core on March 28, 2000, the twister spun off another downtown mixed-use project: The Tower, the $72 million rebirth of the tornado-ravaged but still structurally sound Bank One building. The handsome green-glass skyscraper opened in 2005. By early 2006, its 294 luxury condominiums were nearly sold out. The present focus is on leasing office and retail space.

The urban residential revival moved to the nearby westside in the 1990s, and new development has accelerated since 1999. TRV was a major influence in the 2003 to 2005 stages of redevelopment of the former landmark Montgomery Ward store and warehouse into Montgomery Plaza, a residential, restaurant, and shopping complex anchored by a SuperTarget, part of the national Target discount chain.

Heading south in downtown, developers have restored older buildings that today serve as homes and offices, among other uses. Fort Worth–based XTO Energy, Inc. and other companies relocated to this area, influenced by the city's $75 million renovation of the nearby Fort Worth Convention Center. The city, to enhance its investment, opted for a shared venture with Omni Hotels to build a large, first-class hotel. Construction of the $115 million, 600-room luxury hotel plus parking garage was to begin in 2006. A 2008 opening is expected.

At the south end of downtown, convention-related projects enhanced the nearby Lancaster Avenue Corridor Redevelopment, which features an overhaul of Lancaster Avenue to encourage mixed-use development as well as improvements to the Fort Worth Water Gardens. The corridor's redevelopment took a leap forward with the private-public restoration of the 1930s-vintage Texas & Pacific (T&P) Railroad terminal and its high-rise building. Spring 2006 marked the beginning of sales of condominiums in the T&P's renovated high-rise portion above the railway terminal and in a new mid-rise building next door. The restored terminal portion serves Trinity Railway Express commuter trains, an operation of the Fort Worth Transportation Authority (with Dallas Transit).

Catalysts for Improvements

Real estate development and construction companies serve as catalysts for the renaissance and growth of Fort Worth and Tarrant County. In northern Tarrant and southern Denton counties during the late 1980s, Hillwood Development and its sister companies created the Alliance Texas mixed-use development—which was 17,000 acres in 2006—along Interstate 35W. By early 2006, Alliance Texas encompassed 23.9 million square feet of office, warehouse, factory, and retail space with approximately 140 tenants. Employees working there totaled 24,000. Hillwood has added a luxury hotel and built 5,288 Alliance-area homes in varying price ranges with amenities such as shared parks and outdoor trails.

Among recent industrial tenant ventures, Bell Helicopter is building a $31 million facility. Alliance is earmarked to grow another 120,000 square feet of offices and 1,000 acres of new shopping, including its 600,000-square-foot Alliance Town Center with a 98,000-square-foot JCPenney anchor. Today, the Alliance/Interstate 35W corridor is a popular site among many developers. Nearly 28,000 residents moved into new Alliance-area housing in 2005.

Other Fort Worth–area real estate companies have left their signatures on the region. In the downtown office market sector that improved rapidly during the 1990s, Fort Worth–based Crescent Real Estate Equities Company evolved into one of the nation's largest publicly held real estate investment trusts. Founded here in 1973, Crescent owns and manages, with its subsidiaries and partners, 75 high-end office buildings with a combined 30 million square feet in major metro areas in Texas and seven other states. Its prime downtown Fort Worth investment is the Carter Burgess Plaza skyscraper. Crescent's diversified, capitalized $6 billion real estate investment trust and management portfolio generated 2005 revenues of about $1 billion.

This page: Montgomery Plaza is the finished product of a dramatic facelift of the 1928 catalog store that included carving out a six-story-high passage through the center of the U-shaped building. Opposite page: The redesign of Lancaster Avenue in the south end of downtown will feature art fixtures, grassy medians, and lush landscaping.

PLAZA

W Lancaster

pier 1 impor

Opposite page, top: Alliance Texas, a 17,000-acre, mixed-use, master-planned community in north Fort Worth, includes quality housing in neighborhoods that offer active lifestyles and safe settings. Opposite page, bottom: Pier 1's corporate headquarters is situated on the banks of the Trinity River, just west of Sundance Square. This page: The Trinity River waterfront master plan blends recreational activities with business, retail, and residential development.

One of the area's most prestigious locations, Mercantile Center is a 1,500-acre, master-planned business park with an impressive client list. Another Fort Worth company, N^3 Capital, is a boutique developer of commercial real estate.

Thos. S. Byrne, a general construction contractor, has shaped Fort Worth and vicinity with major area projects since 1923. Byrne partnered with Manhattan Construction Company to build the new Pier 1 Tower on the river. During the 1970s and 1980s, Byrne completed substantial contributions to the Dallas/Fort Worth International Airport and downtown's Sundance Square.

The nation's largest homebuilder, D. R. Horton, also calls Fort Worth home. A Fortune 500 company, D. R. Horton built 51,000 homes in 27 states during fiscal year 2005. Horton opted in 2004 to relocate its headquarters from Arlington to eight leased floors of the 38-story City Center Tower II in downtown Fort Worth. Founded in 1978 in Fort Worth, Horton returned home to take the space vacated when Pier 1 relocated.

Arlington-based Choice Homes, another area construction leader among the top U.S. homebuilders, has built homes in more than 130 Texas and Georgia communities. Founded in 1987, the privately held company is responsible for dozens of housing subdivisions and new developments in the Fort Worth–Dallas Metroplex.

Howard Construction, which is African-American owned, has a history of more than 60 years in Fort Worth. SEDALCO Construction Services is a top firm in contracting and construction management. Reflecting brightly on the booming construction scene, Ajax Glass and Mirror Company provides glass, mirrors, and building hardware for all types of construction.

Midwest Wrecking Company of Texas, Inc. is a top demolition expert, clearing entire buildings or parts thereof for redevelopment and new construction. The company cleared the sites for the RadioShack corporate campus and the Pier 1 headquarters.

For those seeking real estate professionals, Williams Trew Real Estate Services provides full service, including urban, rural, and property management. NAI Huff Partners is the largest commercial real estate firm in Tarrant County.

Indeed, many companies have shared in making Fort Worth a fast-growing people place. Now it's on the cusp of becoming an even better people place on the river.

Please No Strollers
Walk Left Stand Right

Opposite page: With five terminals, the Dallas/Fort Worth International Airport is the busiest in Texas and third-busiest in the world. This page, top: American Airlines, the largest scheduled passenger airline in the world, is based in Fort Worth. This page, bottom: Fort Worth Alliance Airport, considered the world's first purely industrial airport, features an award-winning FAA control tower.

POINT A TO ALL POINTS

Transportation, Distribution, and Warehousing

With a central U.S. location, open spaces, and a mild climate, the Fort Worth–Arlington metropolitan area boasts one of the country's most impressive hubs for transportation, distribution, and warehousing. The area is an international crossroads served by one of the world's busiest airports and airlines. On a national scale, the region has a leading industrial airport and the two largest railroads. All have convenient access to the Gulf of Mexico and Atlantic and Pacific seaports.

Flying High

The Fort Worth–Dallas–Arlington metroplex is home to an upgraded and expanding Dallas/Fort Worth International Airport (DFW), the world's third busiest, which in 2005 channeled nearly 60 million passengers. In 2006 the airport handled nearly 1,900 flights daily to and from approximately 170 U.S. and international destinations. Overall, DFW generates a North Texas regional economic impact of $14 billion annually and was a key factor in more than 400 corporate headquarters relocating to or expanding in the metroplex during the decade ending in 2005.

Air transportation in Tarrant County includes Fort Worth Alliance Airport, which specializes in industrial cargo and corporate air transportation and also provides service to general aviation clientele and all U.S. military branches. Opened in 1989, the airport was a project of the city, the federal government, and AllianceTexas, the latter being a master-planned, mixed-use development in northern Tarrant and southern Denton counties. In 2005 the airport handled 220,134 metric tons of cargo, a 28 percent increase from the prior year.

This page: Fort Worth's expansive system of federal, state, and local highways helps position the city as a major transportation hub. Opposite page: Loop 820 South, just south of downtown, connects Interstates 35W and 20.

At the core of both Fort Worth Alliance and DFW International airports is Fort Worth–based American Airlines, the world's largest airline and a company that has been part of Fort Worth's history since the 1920s.

Its parent company, AMR Corporation, is also headquartered in Fort Worth and is Tarrant County's long-time leading employer, with about 24,300 workers in early 2006. At Alliance Airport, American Airlines operates its state-of-the-art maintenance and engineering base, which employs approximately 2,000 workers. At DFW, American Airlines is a leading carrier with approximately 800 daily departures via American and its American Eagle line to 120 U.S. and foreign destinations.

Other Tarrant County public airports include Fort Worth Meacham International Airport and Fort Worth Spinks Airport. Meacham is a city airport that offers scheduled and chartered passenger flights, corporate flight and general aviation services, student pilot training, and aircraft maintenance, repairs, modifications, and sales. Spinks focuses on providing public general aviation services, flight training, and air ambulance services.

Driven to Perfection

Fort Worth–Arlington's road transportation system is impressive, too. Multiple federal, state, and local highways and byways feed into three critical trade arteries that link the area to Dallas, the nation, and Mexico. The three routes include the north-south Interstate 35W and the east-west Interstate 30 and Interstate 20, both of which are linked with north-south Interstate 45 and its major path to Houston. Critical to the region's economic health, the highway system is undergoing constant improvements, such as adding massive interchanges, land additions, and resurfacing.

Slated for a big slice of those improvements is high-volume Texas 121, a portion of which serves the DFW area in northwest Tarrant. On its south-southwest Tarrant side, Texas 121 will become Southwest Parkway to link Johnson County to the broader metroplex transportation network and to serve a booming population. Toll lanes or roads are planned.

One of the biggest projects is the planned Trans-Texas Corridor (TTC). This includes the Trans-Texas Corridor 35 segment to be built along stretches of existing Interstate 35 and new pathways south from the Oklahoma-Texas state line through the Fort Worth–Dallas metroplex and southward via two potential routes—one to Mexico, and the other along the Texas Gulf Coast. New, high-speed toll roads, upgraded and new highway segments, railroad and utility lines, pipelines, and other elements will be incorporated into this new state network covering more than 4,000 miles.

The Fort Worth region's impressive highway system lends itself to a substantial trucking industry. Among the area's trucking leaders, Fort Worth–based Andrews Transport focuses on hauling bulk—and sometimes hazardous—liquids such as glues, solvents, gasoline, coal tar products, and jet fuel. The company has transit service partnerships worldwide and maintains terminals in Texas, Louisiana, and Oklahoma.

Among the area's largest operators, Con-way, based in San Mateo, California, has its Con-way Freight–Southern branch in Fort Worth. The division specializes in next-day and second-day service across 12 southern states and Puerto Rico, and operates 119 service centers capable of delivering to destinations in more than 25,000 regional cities that link the company to national and global markets.

This page: The Trinity Railway Express, which provides transportation between Fort Worth and Dallas, had more than 2.4 million riders in fiscal year 2006. Opposite page, top: The Fort Worth Intermodal Transportation Center provides access to commuter rail service, national train service, taxis, and buses. Opposite page, below: Headquartered in Fort Worth, Burlington Northern Santa Fe is one of the largest U.S. railroads.

Another leader is Fort Worth–based LoneStar Transportation, which has approximately 800 contractors, agents, and employees focused on flatbed hauling across the 48 contiguous states, Canada, and Mexico. The company is a national leader in hauling for the wind-power industry, with specialized flatbeds carrying huge windmill towers, blades, turbines, and related components.

Mass Transit and Railways

While the area's highway improvements are intended to ease traffic congestion, government agencies and other organizations promote an alternative to driving: rail transit. One of the biggest advocates is the Fort Worth Transportation Authority, which manages an array of transportation modes from a multicity bus system to services for mobility-impaired residents to jointly operating the Trinity Railway Express (TRE) with Dallas Area Rapid Transit. The TRE is the commuter rail service from Fort Worth to Dallas.

Besides commuter transit, rail offers the Fort Worth area excellent cargo transport services. Since the mid 1990s, the nation's two largest railway companies have provided nearly all rail freight for Tarrant County's shippers and receivers. Fort Worth–based Burlington Northern Santa Fe (BNSF) Railway, the second-largest railway in North America, operates its ultra-modern Alliance Logistics Park facility, which includes the BNSF automobile–rail–truck transfer yard; the BNSF freight railcar yard; and the BNSF Intermodal freight-handling hub.

The world's largest rail intermodal operator and volume handler, BNSF in 2005 carried more than five million intermodal shipments. Its large corporate campus in north Fort Worth runs a high-tech control and tracking system that herded record-breaking traffic records in 2006. Tracked and monitored by BNSF dispatchers, about 5,700 locomotives and 220,000 freight cars are operated, though not all daily, across BNSF's 32,000 railroad route miles in 28 states and two Canadian provinces.

Fort Worth's other rail giant is the Omaha, Nebraska–based Union Pacific (UP), Texas's largest railroad with 6,388 miles of tracks. The company operates two rail yards and a diesel locomotive repair shop in Fort Worth. Also a leading intermodal carrier, UP operates across 32,400 miles of tracks in 23 states with gateways to Mexico and Canada. It has 8,000 locomotives and 107,000 freight cars.

Logistically Speaking

From well-connected intermodal services to high-tech business parks, the Fort Worth region is equipped to handle its vast transportation network. BNSF Railway's Intermodal Facility is a prime example, with its access to Alliance Airport runways in Alliance Texas. This intermodal service links with major highways via its site in Logistics Park, Alliance Texas's business park and part of the mixed-use development. With its number of commercial and industrial tenants growing, Alliance has plans for runway extensions, more direct railroad and airport runway access, and increasing warehouse and distribution facilities. Major tenants include FedEx, Bell Helicopter, and Home Depot.

DFW also delivers on logistical support. Airlines at DFW average handling about 250,000 metric tonnes of cargo annually. As Foreign Trade Zone Number 39, the airport has 2,500 acres of direct airfield, railway, and highway access. Altogether, the airport's cargo facilities cover more than 2.6 million square feet, which includes refrigerated storage space, 156 truck dock doors, and ramp parking for eight of the largest cargo aircraft.

The area's transportation industry dovetails with at least eight major business-industrial parks. For instance, Railhead Fort Worth offers more than 630 acres featuring access to the BNSF and UP railroads, Interstate 35W, Fort Worth's inner-belt Loop 820, and short drives to major airports and downtown Fort Worth. Major tenants include International Paper and Mattel.

Opposite page: Dallas/Fort Worth International Airport handles an average of 250,000 metric tonnes of cargo annually. This page: Railhead Fort Worth, a 633-acre industrial park, is the largest industrial center in Fort Worth that offers dual rail service.

Another example is CentrePort, a 1,300-acre development with high-speed fiber optics, underground utilities, security patrol, a fire station, hotel and restaurants, child-care services, and access to the TRE, rail freight, airports, and multiple highways. Tenants include American Airlines, OfficeMax, and Whirlpool.

With Full Support

Fort Worth–Arlington's transportation infrastructure buttresses a strong distribution industry that includes stalwarts such as the Fort Worth–based Ben E. Keith Company, which celebrated its 100th anniversary in 2006. It is the ninth-largest U.S. distributor to the dining-out trade, and a regional leader in distributing refrigerated, fresh, and frozen foods as well as dry groceries, paper goods, equipment, and other supplies to restaurants, hospitals, schools, and other institutional clientele in 10 states. The company's beer division is one of the world's largest distributors of St. Louis, Missouri–based Anheuser-Busch products.

Ben E. Keith is just one of many distribution companies that bolster Fort Worth's intricate transportation network, making the city a key player in today's global economy.

PART THREE
PORTRAITS OF SUCCESS: PROFILES OF COMPANIES AND ORGANIZATIONS

AEROSPACE AND DEFENSE
PROFILES OF COMPANIES AND ORGANIZATIONS

Lockheed Martin Aeronautics Company

Having earned its recognition through relentless research and development of high-performance aircraft and continual pursuit of innovative, low-cost design and manufacturing strategies, this company is known for building some of the world's finest military aircraft—including the F-35 Lightning II joint strike fighter of the future.

Above left: The long list of dependable and highly regarded aircraft made by Lockheed Martin Aeronautics Company includes the F-35 Lightning II (left), which is under development, and the F-22 Raptor (right) air superiority fighter. With its breakthroughs in maneuverability, stealth, and sensor fusion, the Raptor can fight the world's most advanced radar networks and missile environments, defeating air and ground threats, present and future. Above right: The F-16 Fighting Falcon is produced at the company's Fort Worth plant, which is home to the F-16 program.

Lockheed Martin Aeronautics Company is a world leader in the design, research and development, systems integration, production, and support of advanced military aircraft and related technologies. Its customers include the military services of the United States and allied nations throughout the world.

The products of Lockheed Martin Aeronautics include the F-35 Lightning II joint strike fighter, F-22 Raptor air superiority fighter, F-16 Fighting Falcon multirole fighter, F-117 Nighthawk stealth fighter, C-130J Super Hercules and C-5 Galaxy transport aircraft, P-3 Orion and S-3 Viking maritime patrol aircraft, and U-2 reconnaissance and surveillance aircraft. With 14,500 local employees, the company's site on the west side of Fort Worth is its headquarters and the home of the F-16 and F-35 programs. The plant also manufactures portions of the F-22 Raptor and the F-2 fighter for Japan. In addition to its Fort Worth operations, Lockheed Martin Aeronautics has major facilities in Marietta, Georgia, and Palmdale, California.

Lockheed Martin Aeronautics, with $11.7 billion in 2005 sales, is a business area of Lockheed Martin Corporation. Headquartered in Bethesda, Maryland, Lockheed Martin employs about 140,000 people worldwide and is principally engaged in the research, design, development, manufacture, integration, and sustainment of advanced technology systems, products, and services. The corporation reported 2005 sales of $37.2 billion.

Lockheed Martin Aeronautics has a diverse work force that includes thousands of engineers and individuals with advanced degrees, as well as highly skilled manufacturing and aircraft operations specialists. The company is pursuing several initiatives to ensure that it will be able to recruit and retain the kinds of employees it will need for continued success in a highly competitive technical job market. Lockheed Martin products play a critical role in the defense of the United States and allied nations. For example, the F-16 has been used extensively in Iraq and Afghanistan operations and has been in use to safeguard the skies of the United States since September 11, 2001.

More than 7,000 world-renowned military aircraft, from bombers to fighters, have been produced at the Lockheed Martin Aeronautics plant in Fort Worth since it opened in 1942.

Lockheed Martin F-35, Fort Worth

CITY GOVERNMENT

PROFILES OF COMPANIES AND ORGANIZATIONS

City of Fort Worth

With remarkable foresight and planning, city leaders, businesses, and organizations have taken action to re-create Fort Worth as an award-winning metropolis—marshaling forces to create new infrastructure, a vibrant downtown, thousands of jobs, and 'urban villages,' and remake the river—preserving the Old West in a contemporary scene.

Above: At night, the skyline of downtown Fort Worth reflects the community's spirit of contemporary urban revitalization. Consistently ranked among the top places in the nation to work, live, and do business, Fort Worth offers diverse commerce opportunities, good educational resources, and unique attractions—from historic sites to sports, arts, and entertainment.

From a military outpost protecting settlers on the edge of the western frontier in 1849 to a bustling metropolis of more than 661,000 people and the 18th-largest city in the nation as of 2006, the city of Fort Worth is a crossroads of American culture and history.

In 1849, on a high bluff near the point where the Clear Fork and West Fork of the Trinity River meet, Major Ripley Arnold established a fort, named for General William Jenkins Worth, to protect settlers from attacks by native inhabitants. Though the fort was soon abandoned as the western frontier was pushed farther across the continent, the growing town became a stop for cattle drives on the Chisholm Trail.

The arrival of cowboys fresh off the trail led to the development of one of the nation's most infamous red light districts. Dubbed "Hell's Half Acre," the area—in which the Fort Worth Convention Center is located today—was littered with gambling parlors, saloons, and dance halls. The district was propelled into history books as a meeting place for western legends Butch Cassidy and the Sundance Kid.

The Texas and Pacific Railway was connected to Fort Worth in 1876, transforming this stop along the trail into a premier destination for cattle raisers. The advent of refrigerated railroad cars, along with the efforts of local businessmen, soon brought meatpackers to Fort Worth, including two major names—Armour and Swift—earning the industry-leading Fort Worth Livestock Exchange the nickname "Wall Street of the West."

The area around the livestock exchange, now the Fort Worth Stockyards National Historic District, has become a popular tourist attraction and offers entertainment, restaurants, and night life, courtesy of businesses such as the vast entertainment spot Billy Bob's Texas: "The World's Largest Honky Tonk."

The Fort Worth Stock Show and Rodeo, over a century old, is held annually at the Will Rogers Memorial Coliseum in the Fort Worth Cultural District, giving visitors a glimpse of old days, in a family-friendly atmosphere.

The military has always been a major asset in Fort Worth. World War I led the U.S. Department of War in 1917 to create Camp Bowie in west Fort Worth as a training site, and later a demobilization center, before it was closed in 1919.

Built as a training ground for pilots and a site for constructing aircraft during World War II, Tarrant Field Airdrome was renamed Carswell Air Force Base in 1948. It became the headquarters of the 19th Air Division in 1951 and was home to B-52 bombers of the 7th Bomb Wing—a crucial piece of the U.S. nuclear arsenal during the Cold War and of the Strategic Air Command. The airfield's construction facility has witnessed a variety of military aircraft, including the widely used F-16 Fighting Falcon, from various defense contractors—Convair, General Dynamics, and today Lockheed Martin. Repurposed as the Naval Air Station–Joint Reserve Base Fort Worth (NAS-JRB) in the 1990s, the facility, located in northwest Fort Worth, connects the city to its military heritage in a time of diversification and growth.

Reshaping for Future Vitality

As the population shifted into the suburbs after World War II, the resulting decline of the inner city drove city leaders to action. Projects such as the Kimbell Art Museum in 1972; the Amon Carter Museum renovation, completed in 2001; and the construction of a new Fort Worth building for the National Cowgirl Museum and Hall of Fame (formerly housed in Hereford) in 2002 have made Fort Worth's Cultural District the third-largest in the nation. The Fort Worth Convention Center,

Above: Fort Worth's Sundance Square, a 20-block area of restored historic buildings, is a vibrant marketplace offering a mix of restaurants, shopping, theater, movies, music, and more.

Above: A model of the Trinity River Vision Master Plan shows projected development along 88 miles of the river, designed to keep the area beautiful and accessible, assure good water management, and enrich the quality of life for the Fort Worth community. Right: Trinity River Vision involves enhancing the river's recreational resources, which include skating, hiking, cycling, and horseback riding trails, boat docks and fishing areas, parks and playgrounds, and even whitewater rafting chutes.

purchased from Tarrant County in 1997, was expanded in 2003 to handle more visitors and exhibitors. Infusions of capital from prominent citizens and businesses created the popular Sundance Square, a showcase of architecture and shopping, dining, and entertainment that draws back tourists and residents looking for the urban lifestyle.

As of 2005 one of the nation's fastest-growing large cities with a population of more than 600,000, and selected in 2004 by Partners for Livable Communities as one of America's Most Livable Communities, Fort Worth has endured economic changes and retained its western heritage as it continues to prosper.

In 2005 Fort Worth was ranked the ninth-safest large city in the nation by Morgan Quitno, even while experiencing a population boom. Knowing that rapid growth brings with it a responsibility to maintain or better the standard of living, city leaders and investors have taken steps to reshape the urban core, revitalize older neighborhoods, and encourage development designed to eliminate urban sprawl.

Alliance Texas

Located in north Fort Worth, 15 miles northwest of Dallas/Fort Worth International Airport and near Fort Worth Alliance Airport, which specializes in serving industrial aviation, is the 17,000-acre Alliance Texas master-planned commercial and residential community. This development—in the 65-square-mile area that makes up Alliance Texas—houses 140 companies, and 62 of these are ranked among the Fortune 500, the Fortune Global 500, or the *Forbes* list of

top private firms. As of mid 2006, 24,000 workers in 23.9 million square feet of commercial space call the development home; yet only 4,500 acres have been developed of the project's 17,000 total. When complete, the community is projected to include 88 million square feet of commercial space and employ 92,000 workers. Additionally, Alliance Texas will have a residential component with 3,800 single-family homes, 1,500 of which already have been built.

At the center of this development is the pedestrian-oriented, comprehensive mixed-use Alliance Town Center—a first of its kind for north Texas. Future phases will include a grocery store–anchored center and a Main Street component with specialty retail shops on ground level with residential space above.

The Trinity River Vision

The Trinity River is one of Fort Worth's greatest natural assets, intimately tied to both the history and the future of the city.

Though attempts to tame the river following a major flood in the late 1940s left stretches of mere muddy ditches, renewal efforts since then have returned the river to its past glory. A $435 million project to restructure the Trinity River, approved by the federal government, commenced in 2006.

The Trinity River Vision project includes over 88 miles of river and tributaries in the greater Fort Worth area and addresses issues such as flood protection, the environment, recreation, waterfront access, green space, and urban revitalization, thus improving the river's accessibility to the public—attracting more people to its banks and increasing its prominence within the city. Major corporations, educational institutes, and residential developments can already be seen near the river, bringing the city closer to the vision of people living, working, learning, shopping, and playing along its welcoming banks.

Urban Villages

Promoting conscientious growth in already developed areas, the city has designated 16 urban villages throughout Fort Worth as part of a program started in 2001 to create public transportation- and pedestrian-friendly mixed-use communities—allowing businesses and residents to live together comfortably in a compact geographic area.

One such project in the historic neighborhood of Evans and Rosedale will house the Fort Worth Public Health Department and the Shamblee Branch of the Fort Worth Public Library. The newly renovated Tommy Tucker School is a cornerstone of the development, which will include commercial anchors, restaurants, and jazz venues, as well as medical and residential services.

The Sierra Vista project, at the intersection of East Berry and Riverside, represents an effort to revitalize an underserved area. A $3 million upgrade of public infrastructure is projected to leverage $19 million in private investment. The Fort Worth City Council has planned to allot more resources to this development, which will include single-family homes, a retail center, and other venues, and developer Vertex Asset Partners is working with Southeast Fort Worth Inc. in courting major retailers for the subsequent commercial phases.

The face and landscape of Fort Worth is in a constant state of metamorphosis, contributing to the city's already dynamic atmosphere. Local heritage has greatly influenced development in this rising metropolis—ensuring improvements that will let residents and visitors taste the city's unique flavor now and for years to come.

Top: Evans Avenue Public Plaza is designed as a centerpiece of the Evans and Rosedale Business and Cultural District redevelopment project. The city of Fort Worth commissioned a plan to restore the district as a showcase of the city's rich African-American heritage. Above: Lancaster Avenue is being transformed into a broad, attractive thoroughfare with trees, grass, and public art, leading to the development of an urban village.

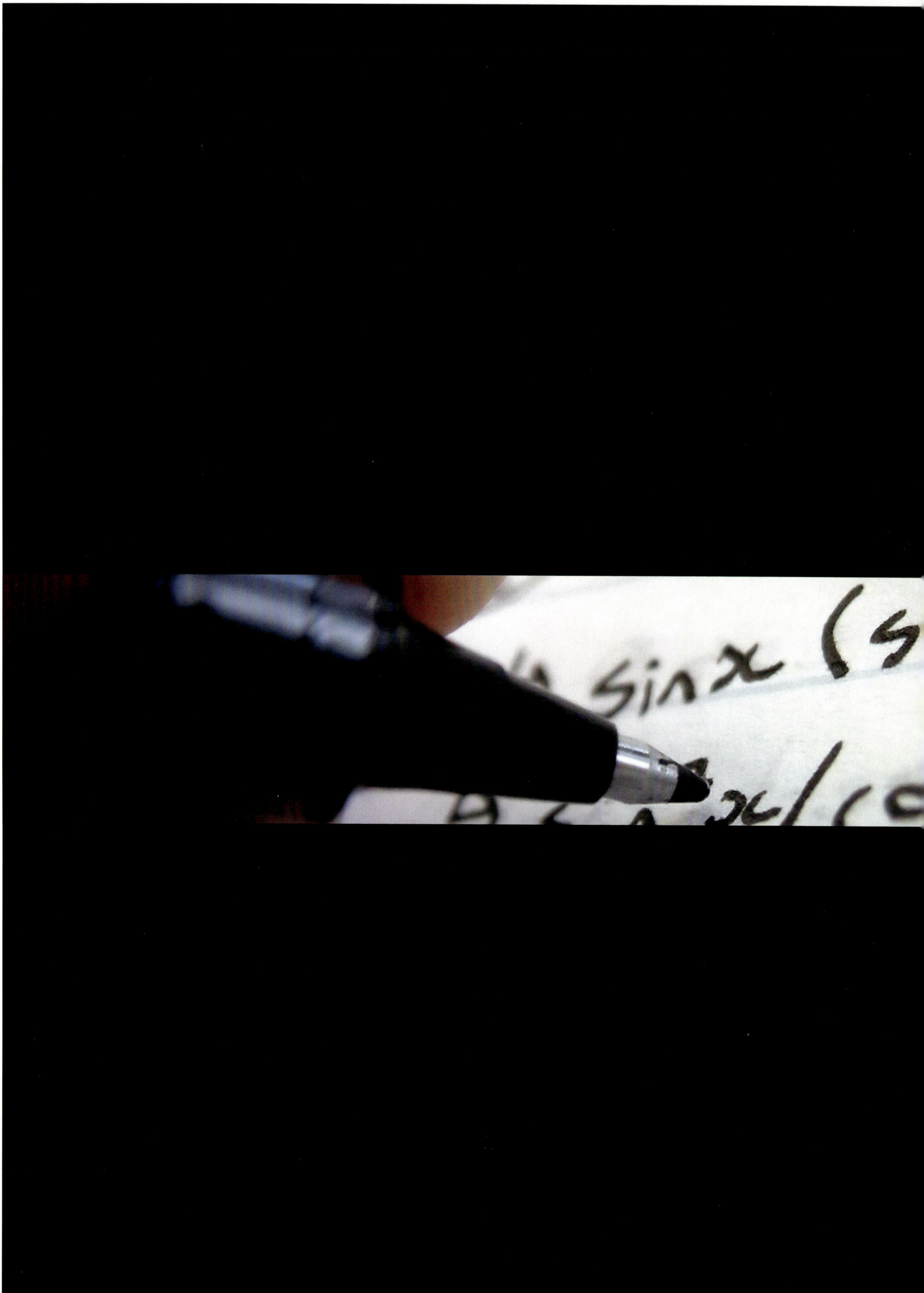

EDUCATION
PROFILES OF COMPANIES AND ORGANIZATIONS

This vibrant and growing center—which emphasizes education, research, patient care, and community service—provides post-graduate training in osteopathic medicine, biomedical science, public health, physician assistant studies, and other health professions.

Above: The University of North Texas Health Science Center at Fort Worth (UNTHSC-FW) is located in the Fort Worth Cultural District.

From the laboratory to the bedside and into the community, the University of North Texas Health Science Center at Fort Worth is helping to shape the future of medicine.

Located in the heart of the Fort Worth Cultural District, the center encompasses the Texas College of Osteopathic Medicine (TCOM), the Graduate School of Biomedical Sciences (GSBS), the School of Public Health (SPH), the Physician Assistant Studies Program (PASP), and the School of Health Professions (SHP), each of which offers small classes, an innovative curriculum, and a collaborative environment for students.

The school was chartered as TCOM in 1966, and accepted its first students in 1970. With the establishment of the GSBS in 1993, the organization became a health science center and its name was changed to University of North Texas Health Science Center at Forth Worth (UNTHSC-FW). The state approved the addition of the SPH in 1995, PASP in 1996, and SHP in 2004.

Today UNTHSC-FW has more than 250 full-time and 550-plus adjunct faculty members. It has a growing annual enrollment of some 1,100 students and an alumni base of more than 3,000. Students may pursue doctoral degrees in Osteopathic Medicine, Biomedical Sciences, or Public Health; master's degrees in Physician Assistant Studies, Biomedical Sciences, or Public Health; or dual degrees.

Leadership

UNTHSC-FW continually receives recognition for its endeavors and collaborations, for example:

- TCOM consistently has been ranked among the top 50 medical schools in the United States for primary care by *U.S.News and World Report* and was named one of the nation's five Best Schools for Hispanics by *Hispanic Business* magazine. TCOM is noted for its leading-edge efforts in curriculum reform, its use of automated simulators for training, and its unique program to prepare primary care physicians to serve the needs of rural Texans. The PASP makes special efforts toward helping to meet the health care needs of medically underserved areas.
- GSBS has received a variety of awards for minority recruitment and science mentoring and ranks among the top schools in the United States in National Institutes of Health (NIH) funding granted per total number of basic science faculty members. The school's master's program in Forensic Genetics is the only one of its type in the nation, and the DNA crime laboratory at the school is the only academic center–based laboratory in the United States qualified to work with the Federal Bureau of Investigation (FBI).
- Research at UNTHSC-FW focuses on a variety of the most challenging medical issues, including aging, Alzheimer's disease, cardiovascular disease, cancer, vision problems, diabetes, health disparities, and more. The center is home to the National Osteopathic Research Center, and it is one of only six institutions to be named by the NIH as a Center on Health Disparities Research. Collaboration is critical to the research efforts of the center, which has ongoing partnerships within the University of Texas

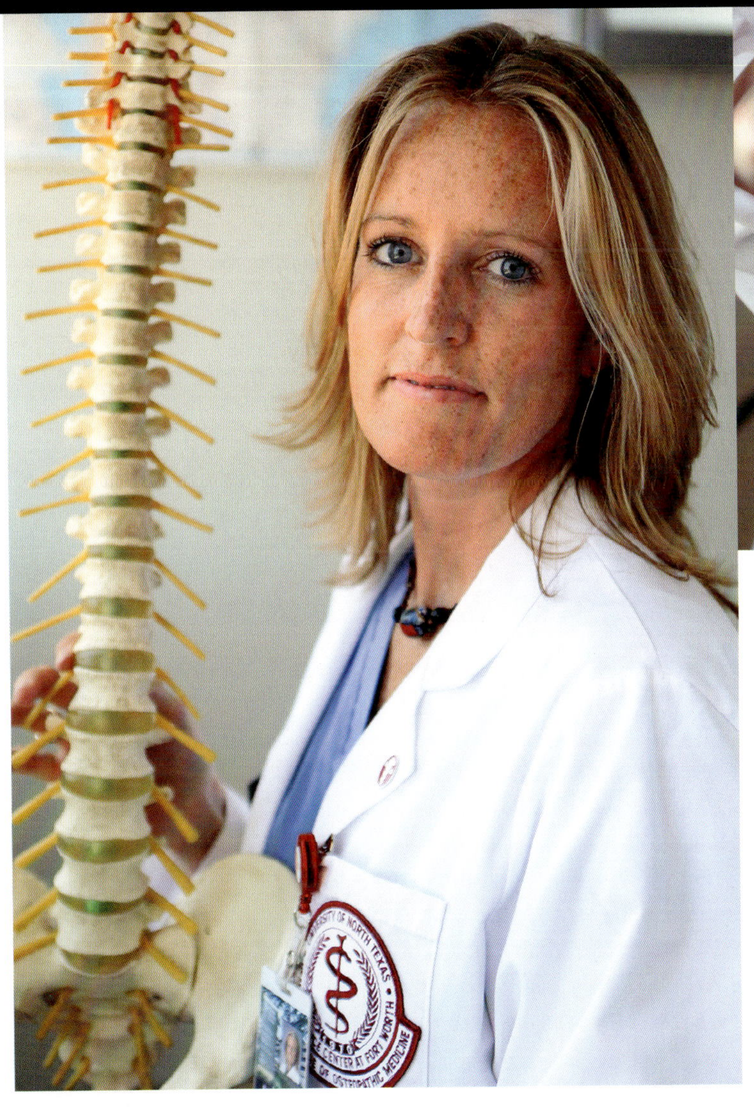

system and with other area universities, as well as with health science centers abroad.

- SPH is one of 37 accredited schools of public health in the United States, and one of only three in Texas. It has been ranked 19th of the more than 300 graduate programs in community health by *U.S.News and World Report.*

Reaching Out

Physician faculty members of TCOM take the knowledge shared in the classroom into the community as UNT Health, the physician group practice. This group represents the expertise of both osteopathic and allopathic medicine and is one of the largest multispecialty group physician practices in Fort Worth. On campus and in clinics and hospitals across the area, these physicians bring the latest advances in medicine to the people of Tarrant County.

Community service is part of UNTHSC-FW's mission. The center helped found and continues to support the annual Cowtown Marathon—Fort Worth's 12,000-athlete road race—and the annual Hispanic Wellness Fair, which is attended by some 15,000 people. Students, faculty, and staff also work with more than 10 school outreach programs at all levels, as well as with teachers, to extend the knowledge of health and healing beyond the campus.

With the purchase of neighboring land formerly occupied by the Osteopathic Medical Center of Texas, UNTHSC-FW doubled the size of its campus in 2005 and is substantially expanding its programs and student enrollment to provide even more health professionals for Texas and the nation.

Left: The Texas College of Osteopathic Medicine —one of the esteemed colleges and schools of UNTHSC-FW— is the only accredited osteopathic medical school in Texas. A majority of its graduates enter primary-care residency programs. Above: Research at UNTHSC-FW is conducted using state-of-the-art instrumentation, and programs continue to advance rapidly.

Southwestern Baptist Theological Seminary

This seminary offers theological education for individuals engaging in Christian ministry, providing undergraduate and graduate curricula in a community designed to develop spiritual leaders with the skills to minister effectively in a rapidly changing world.

Founded by B. H. Carroll in 1908, Southwestern Baptist Theological Seminary moved to Fort Worth in 1910 and settled on one of Tarrant County's highest points, which was quickly dubbed "Seminary Hill." Located a few miles from the city's historic stockyards and infamous "Hell's Half Acre" downtown, the seminary changed the religious landscape of the city.

Carroll served as president of the school until his death in 1914. Other presidents have been L. R. Scarborough, E. D. Head, J. Howard Williams, Robert E. Naylor, Russell H. Dilday, and Kenneth S. Hemphill. Paige Patterson serves as the seminary's eighth president.

Southwestern's School of Theology offers graduate degrees in the pastoral, preaching, and teaching disciplines. Graduates normally serve as pastors, professors of theology, missionaries, or as denominational leaders. The school is home to the Center for Theological Research and the Center for Expository Preaching.

The Roy Fish School of Evangelism and Missions offers graduate degrees to students for service as career missionaries, evangelists, and professors.

The School of Church Music houses the Kathryn Sullivan Bowld Music Library, which maintains more than 30,000 books, 19,000 recordings, 200,000 octavios, and 108,500 scores. The school is also home to the Southwestern Oratorio Chorus and sponsors the annual gala concert of sacred music at Bass Performance Hall in downtown Fort Worth.

The School of Educational Ministries teaches the philosophy and principles of religious education. The school offers graduate degrees in counseling, youth ministry, communications, administration, and children's ministry.

The College at Southwestern offers a baccalaureate degree program in Bible and the history of Western ideas. Students are introduced to the history and development of Western thought in order to learn how to minister in their rapidly changing cultural climate.

Southwestern also offers theological education at its campuses in Houston, San Antonio, Marshall, and Plano, Texas; in Little Rock, Arkansas; and in Shawnee, Oklahoma.

The Association of Theological Schools, the Southern Association of Colleges and Schools, and the National Association of Schools of Music all accredit the seminary and its distance-learning programs. Southwestern alumni serve as pastors, teachers, music and youth ministers, counselors, military and hospital chaplains, and missionaries around the globe. The sun never sets on Southwestern.

Above left: The B. H. Carroll Memorial Building, with central rotunda, is a hallmark of the main campus of Southwestern Baptist Theological Seminary in Fort Worth, Texas. Above right: The seminary community gathers three times a week during semesters for worship in Truett Auditorium.

Texas Christian University (TCU)

A major teaching and research university, TCU offers rigorous academic programs, 100 undergraduate majors and 20 graduate degrees. Reflecting its liberal arts heritage, TCU addresses significant questions of meaning and values, yet also assures its graduates are well prepared for professional careers.

Texas Christian University (TCU) and Fort Worth have been partners since 1911. Both represent the "New Texas" and are vibrant, globally oriented, and on the move. Recognizing this partnership and TCU's unique contributions to the city, the Fort Worth Chamber of Commerce honored the university with its 2006 Spirit of Enterprise Award.

That enterprising spirit began with TCU's forerunner, AddRan Male & Female College, founded in 1873 in tiny Thorp Spring, Texas. TCU has since grown into a major comprehensive university, producing graduates intent on changing the world.

TCU delivers a world-class, values-centered university experience. Consistently ranked in the top 5 percent of the 3,500 universities and colleges in the nation, TCU annually exceeds enrollment goals. Its billion-dollar endowment is among the top 60 college and university endowments in the United States.

TCU students have many of the benefits found at large universities. They can choose from 100 undergraduate majors and can participate in innovative programs such as entrepreneurship and nurse anesthesia. Their professors are leaders in their fields, and academic offerings are rigorous. Classes are taught with a global perspective, and students have numerous opportunities to study abroad.

Since 2000, TCU has invested some $200 million in top-of-the-line facilities, and its ambitious building program continues. Designed to strengthen the TCU experience, the $100 million Campus Commons, slated to open in 2008, comprises the Brown-Lupton University Union, four new residence halls, and an expansive greenscape. The $11.5 million Mabee Foundation Education Complex, to be completed in 2007, will enable TCU to even more effectively tackle key educational issues and prepare teachers for North Texas and beyond. A new indoor practice field will benefit Fort Worth's "home teams"—including the top 25–ranked, NCAA Division IA Horned Frog football team, one of TCU's three conference championship teams.

TCU is the largest of 18 colleges and universities associated with the Christian Church (Disciples of Christ), a community embracing both faith and reason. With the full support of the Disciples, TCU is committed to the highest standard of scholarship, affording students the rigorous challenges that make higher education worthwhile.

With a 14-to-one student-faculty ratio and a teacher-scholar model that results in close, mentoring relationships, the university offers many of the advantages of smaller liberal arts colleges. "That's why a TCU education is not just the sum of semester hours," observes Chancellor Victor J. Boschini, Jr. "It's an entire experience that grows from our mission: 'to educate individuals to think and act as ethical leaders and responsible citizens in the global community.'"

Above left: The Texas Christian University (TCU) campus encompasses 268 acres five miles from the heart of downtown Fort Worth. Since 2000, the university has invested some $200 million in building new facilities and in upgrading residence halls, classrooms, and laboratories. Above right: With an enrollment of more than 8,800, TCU attracts students from 49 states and 85 nations. Each year, members of a TCU class together tackle one of the elements of the mission statement, "to educate individuals to think and act as ethical leaders and responsible citizens in the global community."

The University of Texas at Arlington/ Fort Worth Higher Education Center

Offering affordable credit courses and continuing education opportunities to the communities of Fort Worth and broader Tarrant County, this branch of the world-class University of Texas at Arlington gives its students the knowledge and skills to succeed in their choice of academic disciplines and in their professions.

Above: "The Center's innovative Master in Business Administration (MBA) Cohort program was designed with help from the business community, with the demands of the business community in mind," says John Shellene, a Cohort MBA graduate and a Fort Worth Center Advisory Council member. Right: The University of Texas at Arlington/ Fort Worth Higher Education Center (the Center) is expanding its presence by subleasing the Santa Fe Freight Building in downtown Fort Worth. This location, which will be operational in spring 2007, will serve as the Center's new headquarters.

The University of Texas at Arlington/ Fort Worth Higher Education Center (the Center) provides the opportunity for undergraduates to earn a Bachelor of Business Administration (BBA) in Management through its collaboration with Tarrant County College; it also provides complete graduate programs in four disciplines. The Center is currently located at Riverbend Park in Fort Worth, which is also home to the Automation and Robotics Research Institute.

In 2000, the Center's first Master in Business Administration (MBA) Cohort program enrolled 42 students. With the addition of master's programs in Health Care Administration and Educational Leadership (both in 2001), in Engineering Management (2003), and in Systems Engineering (2005), the Center has grown to serve more than 850 students.

This increase in enrollment has allowed the Center to broaden its educational offerings. The Center will also expand its geographic presence by subleasing the Santa Fe Freight Building in downtown Fort Worth. A major factor in choosing the Santa Fe Freight Building as the Center's new facility and headquarters was the building's ideal location; it is adjacent to the Intermodal Transportation Center, which serves as a downtown hub for bus and train service. At this new facility, the Center will offer graduate level and continuing education courses. The Center will also continue to offer programming at its Riverbend Park location.

The Center, in partnership with Tarrant County College, will also continue its BBA in Management program, which is currently offered at Tarrant County College's Northeast and Northwest campuses.

"The University of Texas at Arlington is always seeking to form new partnerships and new ways in which to serve our communities," says UT Arlington President James D. Spaniolo. "These partnerships will bring new economic life to our beautiful new facility as well as expand higher education opportunities in downtown Fort Worth."

"We are delighted that the University of Texas System approved the Santa Fe building sublease, and that it plans to bring quality educational opportunities to downtown residents and businesses," says Carter Burdette, chairman of the Downtown Fort Worth Tax Increment Finance District Board of Directors. "This is another important step in the revitalization of the center city."

In addition to credit programming and postgraduate continuing education, the Center provides community outreach. One such initiative is its Distinguished Faculty Lecture Series. In partnership with the Fort Worth Independent School District, this lecture series focuses on a secondary school audience. It brings some of the university's most honored faculty members—from its colleges of Liberal Arts, Science, Business, Education, and Engineering and its schools of Nursing and Social Work—to classrooms throughout the district to encourage all students to continue their education beyond high school.

And in January 2005, The University of Texas at Arlington/Fort Worth Higher Education Center, in conjunction with its alumni chapter, organized the Leadership Professional Network Series. This program is designed to give students and alumni an opportunity to enhance their knowledge and personal skills through a series of development seminars. Topics include conflict management, team building, and leadership. Through its innovative programs and community service, the Center is quickly gaining recognition as an important link in the state's educational system.

ENERGY

PROFILES OF COMPANIES AND ORGANIZATIONS

XTO Energy Inc.

XTO Energy Inc. produces more than 2 percent of the U.S. natural gas volume every day of every year. Based in Fort Worth, this highly successful company complements its entrepreneurial vision with its proven strategies.

From the company's very beginning in 1986, XTO Energy's primary focus was clear: to develop purely domestic, unconventional, and long-lived natural gas and oil plays onshore. After following this focus for 20 years, the company today ranks as the eighth largest natural gas producer in the United States.

Bob R. Simpson, XTO Energy CEO, states, "We never really set a goal of being a 'large' anything. We just wanted to buy quality properties, work with good people, and create value." And if XTO's recent history is any indication, the company is doing exactly that. Since XTO's initial public offering in 1993, this company has outpaced its competitors with shares increasing fortyfold. In 2005, XTO reported 66.4 percent total returns, and an 80 percent increase in revenue over 2004.

Proven Strategy Equals Solid Results

XTO's success is grounded in a proven strategy of low-risk and high returns. The company acquires properties with long production histories that have the potential to continue to produce oil and gas for future years. Typically, these properties have been productive for decades, and more importantly, are expected to continue to be so for many more years.

XTO's advantage comes by hand-picking properties—usually quality source rock that is undermanaged and in need of technology improvements.

Left: Bob R. Simpson—founder, chairman, and CEO of XTO Energy Inc.—has committed a 30-year career to building one of the most successful energy companies on Wall Street. His commitment to his team, his community, and his disciplined business strategy has rewarded stockholders with a 3,700 percent return since XTO went public in 1993. Opposite page: The home for XTO Energy is the famed W. T. Waggoner Building on Houston Street. When completed in 1919, this historic treasure was the tallest building west of the Mississippi. XTO has restored the downtown tower to its original grandeur.

XTO then relies on its team of expert geoscientists to develop the hidden value in these properties. Using the newest tools, along with innovative solutions, XTO is able to increase production and reserves. The result is an ongoing program of growth via low-risk development activities, such as recompletions and development drilling, and increasing opportunities.

Inevitably, the company's properties outperform production estimates while generating excess cash flow to expand the asset base. The results speak for themselves: between 1986 and 2005, XTO acquired 5.5 trillion cubic feet of gas equivalent and, to date, has almost doubled those reserves, creating immense value along the way.

The Power of Three

Originally called Cross Timbers Oil Company, XTO Energy was formed in the spring of 1986 by three former employees from Southland Royalty Company of Fort Worth. The mission of these three visionaries—current CEO Bob Simpson, Jon Brumley, and Steve Palko—was to acquire the best oil and gas properties and make them better, much better. The company began with eight employees and approximately $20 million. By summer, the company had its first modest acquisition—seven non-operated wells in Jones County, Texas. From there, the company acquired the Ringwood Division of Ladd Petroleum Corporation, and the foundation for XTO's burgeoning acquisition model was established.

The company grew at a bold pace. By 1990, XTO had opened additional offices in Midland and Perryton, Texas, as well as in Oklahoma City and Elk City, Oklahoma.

Decades of Change, Acquisitions, and Growth

With significant assets in hand, Cross Timbers went public in May 1993. The initial public offering of 6.7 million shares raised more than $85 million, and the New York Stock Exchange symbol "XTO" was born.

By 1996, XTO held a stronger position in the Permian Basin and had an entry into the famed Hugoton Field, and Bob Simpson was elected chairman of XTO. Under his stewardship, the company aggressively began to pursue natural gas assets.

Above: XTO is the largest producer of natural gas in East Texas and currently ranks as the second largest producer in the state. The company is one of the most active drillers in the nation, with more than 70 active rigs, completing 1,000 prolific wells annually.

In 1997, XTO purchased assets totaling $252 million in the San Juan Basin of northwestern New Mexico from Amoco Corporation. A year later, it acquired $265 million of east Texas properties from EEX Corporation, and $46 million in oil assets in Alaska's Cook Inlet from Shell. In 1999, XTO bought more than $460 million in properties in the Arkoma Basin in Arkansas from the Spring Holding Company and Ocean Energy Inc. Despite the economic downturn in 1998 and 1999, the company continued to follow its strategy of building an inventory of low-risk, high-margin assets.

The growth from these numerous acquisitions solidified XTO's position as a major force in the domestic natural gas arena. In recognition of its new diversified role, the company changed its name from Cross Timbers Oil Company to XTO Energy Inc.

As energy prices rose, XTO, with its strong asset base, began to lead the natural gas sector in both growth and economic returns. Between 2001 and 2005, it acquired more than $4 billion in producing assets, including core areas in east and west Texas and the San Juan Basin. It also carved new core regions in the Rockies and the Barnett Shale of north Texas. The company's stock price matched the tremendous growth, climbing 436 percent over the same period.

XTO Energy in the Present and Future

Today, with almost 2,000 employees, XTO is the fourth largest independent owner of domestic natural gas reserves. The company continues to follow its successful strategy and entrepreneurial approach of acquiring and developing quality, long-lived oil and gas producing properties throughout the United States. From coal bed methane production to tight gas, to shale, to oil, XTO has built a production base that is positioned to create value while pursuing growth. The company currently owns interests in 18,863 wells in Texas, New Mexico, Oklahoma, Arkansas, Kansas, Utah, Louisiana, Colorado, Wyoming, Mississippi, and Alaska.

According to Simpson, XTO makes a practice of replacing its production and reserves with less than 30 percent of cash flow, leaving 70 percent to purchase more production and more shares and to pay dividends. "That is real value creation and gives us the power and flexibility to outperform the sector and overdeliver value," states Simpson. Wall Street has responded to XTO's performance during its 13 years as a public company. From the IPO, the company's stock has grown by more than 3,700 percent.

XTO extends that same dedication to its role as a responsible corporate citizen. The company not only is a major contributor to dozens of organizations—including the National Multiple Sclerosis Association, the Komen Tarrant Race for the Cure, the Gladney Center for Adoption, and the Big Brothers/Big Sisters of North Texas—it also encourages employees to volunteer and participate in community service activities. The company has also committed to revitalizing historic buildings in downtown Fort Worth as part of its commitment to the community.

Simpson concludes, "At XTO Energy, whether it is in business or in the community, we have made exceptional performance a habit. It's driven by a proven strategy, a culture of excellence, and a vision for the future."

'I'll Be Back'

Shortly after forming XTO Energy, company founders purchased a bronze statue by artist Jack Bryant. Titled *I'll Be Back,* the statue depicts a rambunctious cowboy on horseback being run out of town. The cowboy has a fist raised defiantly in the air. The company founders felt that this bronze, purchased at a March of Dimes fundraiser, reflected the courage, strength, and competitive spirit of the newly formed Cross Timbers Oil Company.

I'll Be Back became a mascot of sorts for the company. To this day, replica statues are given to employees as recognition for five years of service.

12/09

FINANCIAL AND INSURANCE SERVICES
PROFILES OF COMPANIES AND ORGANIZATIONS

bank takes pride in providing its customers with quality financial products and responsive personal service, while also working to enhance and strengthen the communities it serves.

Above: Shown here are Citizens National Bank principals, from left, J. Douglas Sanders, executive vice president; and Raymond G. Dickerson, president and CEO.

Since opening in 1986, Citizens National Bank has focused on meeting the banking needs of its customers. Its founders realized that there was a place in Fort Worth and Tarrant County for a locally owned and managed community bank that would provide its employees with a productive working environment, maximize shareholder value, and support programs that would enhance the communities it served.

Reflecting that commitment is the bank's motto: "Real People – Real Solutions." Its staff has earned a reputation for building and keeping relationships. Citizens seeks to exceed its customers' expectations by being flexible, accommodating, and creative. Its customers know that the bank's experienced staff will provide prompt answers to their requests, come up with solutions to avoid problems, and take advantage of opportunities. For example, when individuals or businesses seek loans, the bank helps them assess their options so that they can determine the most cost-effective way to proceed.

Through the years, Citizens has grown by attracting customers who like its approach to banking. They include individuals and professionals with personal and commercial banking needs, as well as businesses with their particular requirements and those of their employees. Citizens' business customers are involved in industries such as manufacturing, construction, real estate, and energy. Its professional customers include physicians, dentists, attorneys, CPAs, financial consultants and planners, and veterinarians. Business owners, entrepreneurs, and investors are a part of the bank's family of customers too.

Citizens offers traditional services such as online banking, checking and savings accounts, certificates of deposit (CDs), money market funds, and home mortgages. In addition, loans are available for residential interim construction, commercial real estate, working capital, Small Business Administration (SBA) 504 loans (real estate and equipment), SB-7A term loans, third-party commercial loans, and revolving lines of credit.

Citizens has an experienced leadership team. Coupled with a seasoned staff, its board of directors is composed of veteran business executives: Raymond G. Dickerson, Citizens' president and CEO, and J. Douglas Sanders, Citizens' executive vice president, are joined by directors Kenneth L. Barr, principal, Kenneth Barr Consulting; James E. Baxter, chairman and president,

Baxter Fentriss and Company; Malinda R. Crumley, Realtor, Brants Realtors; Michael J. McMahon, president, the Gladney Center for Adoption; H. Gray Mills, president, Mills Financial Group, Inc.; Charles H. Newman, chairman of the board, Beadles, Newman & Lawler; Dennis R. Opitz, managing partner, Rylander, Clay & Opitz, LLP; Jerry W. Pozez, owner, Poz-co Development; George H. Sullivan, M.D.; and John W. Wright, managing director, Baxter Fentriss and Company.

Citizens is committed to enhancing the organizations that strengthen the fabric of the communities it serves. It is proud to be the presenting sponsor of the Fort Worth Chamber of Commerce's annual Small Business of the Year Award. The bank has professional and civic memberships in organizations including the Tarrant County Bankers Association, Texas Bankers Association, Texas Independent Bankers Association, Downtown Fort Worth Inc., and chambers of commerce in the area. Its employees are active volunteers for their churches and for many educational, human service, health care, and arts organizations.

For additional information, phone 817-731-1444; visit the bank's Web site at www.citizensnationalbank.com; or visit one of its conveniently located Citizens banking centers: in Fort Worth at 2720 West 7th Street; in Cityview at 6002 Southwest Boulevard at Bryant Irvin Road; in Mansfield at 2170 Matlock Road at Country Club Drive; and in Mid-Cities at 6305 Precinct Line Road at Mid-Cities Boulevard.

Above: Citizens National Bank directors shown here are, from left, Michael J. McMahon, H. Gray Mills, Kenneth L. Barr, and Dennis R. Opitz. Left: The bank's directors include, from left, Jerry W. Pozez, Malinda R. Crumley, and George H. Sullivan, M.D.

credit union and in 2006 became a mutual savings bank serving individual and business customers with comprehensive checking, savings, and lending options and mortgage, financial, and business services.

Above left: OmniAmerican Bank was originally a credit union founded at Carswell Air Force Base, now the Naval Air Station/ Joint Reserve Base (NAS/JRB), located in Fort Worth. Above right: OmniAmerican staff members are shown in this historic photograph, circa 1960s.

OmniAmerican changed Fort Worth's financial landscape in 1956 when seven pioneering military officers contributed $5 each and formed a financial institution to serve personnel stationed at Carswell Air Force Base. Their combined $35 has grown to $1.5 billion in assets under management, while OmniAmerican Bank, originally chartered as Carswell Federal Credit Union, became the institution of choice for customers worldwide.

True to Fort Worth's unique "Cowboys and Culture" environment, OmniAmerican effectively mixes traditional down-home customer service with sophisticated banking options. Enjoying a story and sharing a friendly cup of coffee remains part of the customer experience at a branch office and complements the contemporary convenience of round-the-clock Omni E-Banking.

Since 1956

In 1956, North Texans were listening to radio station KLIF, "The Mighty 1190," and to Doris Day singing "Que Sera, Sera" ("Whatever Will Be, Will Be"), while watching OmniAmerican shape its destiny by design. Over the next decade, OmniAmerican added services and employees. In 1961 OmniAmerican created the organization's first "Loan Officer" staff position (the maximum loan amount at the time was $750).

"Houston, Tranquility Base here. The Eagle has landed." When astronaut Neil Armstrong spoke those words from the moon in 1969, all systems were "go" as OmniAmerican reached two big milestones: serving more than 10,000 customers and managing more than $5 million in assets.

In 1975, while television was airing The Six Million Dollar Man and inflation was at 14 percent, OmniAmerican achieved tremendous growth and value. By the middle of the decade it had more than 19,000 customers and nearly $18 million in assets under management. Car loans, savings and checking accounts, and certificates of deposit met the needs for customers' basic financial services.

By 1984 Fort Worth became a leader in computer development as seen in the top-selling IBM PC-compatible Tandy 1000 computer. Computer circuitry also helped OmniAmerican become a leader in providing 24-hour access to funds. By installing its first Mpact ATM in 1983, OmniAmerican demonstrated the market foresight to establish itself as an unparalleled leader in banking. Before the end of the decade, OmniAmerican would pioneer the use of high-speed fiber-optic communications lines, unveil a new ATM system, and celebrate the opening of the 100,000th account.

"Transition" was the name of the game in the 1990s. In sports, Texas Rangers' pitching legend Nolan Ryan threw the final two of his record seven no-hitters before retiring from baseball in 1993; that same year, the Dallas Stars ice hockey team was welcomed to Dallas from Minnesota.

At OmniAmerican, Larry E. Duckworth was introduced as president and CEO in 1990 to lead the institution into the next century. OmniAmerican exhibited unprecedented growth with the opening of eight additional brick-and-mortar locations and the establishment of telephone banking and electronic banking. New departments, such as Mortgage Lending and Business/Commercial Services, were added so OmniAmerican could serve the entire community. Carswell Federal Credit Union became OmniAmerican Federal Credit Union in 1992.

Today

Since 2000, OmniAmerican has taken two progressively significant steps designed to ensure its next 50 years are as productive as its first: in 2001 OmniAmerican Federal Credit Union members voted to become a state-chartered credit union; and in 2005, OmniAmerican Credit Union members overwhelmingly approved a change for the institution to become a mutual savings bank, thus assuring the continued growth of what is now OmniAmerican Bank.

The bank operates 17 full-service branches, located in Fort Worth, Grapevine, Euless, Arlington, Watauga, Las Colinas, Lewisville, Granbury, Cleburne, Weatherford, and Dallas, and provides electronic banking services and additional information on its Web site (www.OmniAmerican.com). Its headquarters is in Fort Worth.

While Fort Worth has grown from the stockyards to stock cars, and "Cowtown" is now downtown, OmniAmerican has integrated "high touch" with high tech for an uncompromising customer-service experience. And OmniAmerican continues to prove great dreams result in great accomplishments. No crystal balls are needed to see OmniAmerican Bank will continue to provide more services to more people in more ways and to honor its traditions of community responsibility, innovative product offerings, and outstanding customer service.

Above left: For five decades, OmniAmerican Bank branch lobbies have been a place to catch up on news and transact business. Top right: Military and commercial pilots, as well as private citizens, were attracted to OmniAmerican, a financial institution founded by military officers. Above right: OmniAmerican Bank headquarters is proudly located in Fort Worth, Texas.

into Texas. Today, it operates more than 160 banking centers in the Lone Star State, 68 of which are in the Dallas–Fort Worth metropolitan area.

Above: Brian Happel, Fort Worth market president and Tarrant County corporate banking manager, is optimistic about the future of Compass Bank in this region.

Compass Bank succeeds on doing business in an unconventional way—and that is exactly the way its loyal customers want it. The aptly named Compass Bank was founded on the philosophy of driving banking in a new direction, and it is this philosophy that continues to guide this leading financial institution.

For Compass Bank—a subsidiary of the southwestern financial holding company Compass Bancshares, Inc.—being as "un-bankish" as possible means giving customers real, tangible differences. Providing free ATMs and rebating the ATM fees that other banks charge, staying open on holidays when other financial institutions are closed, and ensuring that real—not virtual—bank employees are always available to help customers with their banking needs are just the beginning of the tangible Compass Bank differences.

Overall, Compass Bank combines its intense concentration of expertise and its expansive diversification of services with its long-standing commitment to make banking a unique, personal experience at every turn. It is significant that the Compass Bank experience is underscored by the fact that its employees are local citizens who want to help their communities grow and improve. These Compass Bank employees—like their employer—have a vested interest in their communities.

Charting a New Course

Compass Bank first opened its doors in 1964 as Central Bank of the South in Birmingham, Alabama. Over the years, it grew and expanded through numerous mergers and acquisitions. After the approval of interstate banking in 1987, Central Bank was the first out-of-state bank holding company to enter the Lone Star State.

By 1993, the bank's total assets in Texas alone exceeded $1 billion. That same year, Central Bank changed its name to Compass Bank to reflect the growing diversity of the company and to unify its identity.

Today, Compass Bank is proud to call Texas home to 162 of its

409 branches, with 68 of that significant number in the Dallas–Fort Worth area. Approximately $9.8 billion—or 43 percent—of Compass Bank's total deposits are located in Texas, making it the fourth-largest bank in the Dallas–Fort Worth metropolitan area. Based on its deposit market share, Compass Bank is the fifth-largest in the state.

"Compass Bank is proud to have such a strong presence in North Texas, especially in the Fort Worth and Tarrant County market," says Brian Happel, Compass Bank's Fort Worth market president and Tarrant County corporate banking manager. "We see this as a great opportunity to continue our community investment, and to continue to make this region a great place in which to live and work."

Leading the Banking Industry

Corporate Banking, Retail Banking, and Wealth Management are the three primary lines of business of Compass Bank. Its Corporate Banking division provides a full array of banking and investment services to business banking, commercial banking, and other institutional clients. Retail Banking services address the needs of consumer and small-business customers through Compass Bank's 409 full-service banking centers throughout its six-state footprint. Its Retail Banking division also encompasses online and telephone banking.

Through its Wealth Management Group, Compass Bank provides specialized portfolio management, traditional credit products, financial counseling, and customized services to private clients and foundations.

Pointing out that its parent company, Compass Bancshares, Inc. is among the top 30 U.S. bank holding companies based on asset size, Happel says, "We have all the capabilities of a larger bank, but we are able to deliver them with the personal service and style of a community bank. Compass Bank is everything you could want in a financial partner."

Leading as a Corporate Citizen

Compass Bank's commitment extends beyond its financial expertise to its contributions to the community as a whole. Compass Bank's title sponsorship of Texas Christian University (TCU)'s Texas Youth Entrepreneur of the Year Award and the vast amount of volunteer time donated by the bank to the TCU Neeley Entrepreneurship Program are two of many such examples. In addition, within the Fort Worth community, Compass Bank executives have held leadership positions in the Fort Worth Chamber of Commerce, United Way, and a multitude of other community organizations.

Regional president of Compass Bank–Texas Doug Hutt reflects, "For Compass to be a good corporate citizen, we must recognize and fulfill our responsibility to invest in the communities where we work and live. Our corporate efforts, coupled with the significant volunteer commitment of our employees, enable Compass to meet the financial and social needs of the communities that support us."

It is these sound financial and community investments that have established the present leadership of Compass Bank, and will ensure its continued success into the future.

Above: Doug Hutt, regional president of Compass Bank–Texas, values the bank's opportunities to be a strong supporter of the community.

National Farm Life Insurance Company

With personal service a top priority, this capital stock insurance company—with almost $2 billion of life insurance in force throughout the state—writes, exclusively, life insurance policies. Established in 1946 to benefit farmers and other agriculture workers, the company today serves all Texas residents.

National Farm Life Insurance Company began modestly in 1946 and became the largest Texas-based life insurance company that markets only to Texas residents. National Farm Life provides high quality insurance coverage at the lowest possible cost.

William C. "Brigham" Young founded the company in Fort Worth to provide life insurance for professional agriculture workers. He started in an office borrowed from a friend, and soon moved his growing company into the original Stockyards National Bank, located in Fort Worth's historic stockyards. National Farm Life expanded in the 1950s to extend its services to all Texas residents. Even though the company has now expanded its urban market, a substantial percentage of National Farm Life's policyholders still live in rural areas.

Below: In 1949 the National Farm Life Insurance Company opened its first office in Fort Worth's historic stockyards. Right: During the Christmas and holiday season, National Farm Life's headquarters gets a festive makeover.

In 1968 National Farm Life moved its home office to the east side of Fort Worth, to a 20-acre tract near the interstate highway that links the city to Dallas. Even residents and visitors unfamiliar with National Farm Life probably know the company's building well; it sits atop a hill on Bridge Street, just north of Interstate 30. For many Fort Worth residents, the building symbolizes the Christmas spirit and the holidays. When National Farm Life held its open house and ribbon-cutting ceremony in 1968, it decorated its building with a red bow and streaming red ribbons, which gave the building the appearance of a giant present. The ribbons and bow became a tradition, and the building became a landmark for commuters and travelers along the Dallas–Fort Worth interstate. Every holiday season, National Farm Life meticulously drapes six red ribbons, each 54 feet long and four feet wide, over the building and hoists a giant, 350-pound, 22-foot-long red bow above the front entrance.

Success Founded on Stability

National Farm Life has more than $240 million in assets. A. M. Best Company, an independent insurance industry analyst, gives National Farm Life an A- (excellent) for its overall financial condition.

Since 1946, National Farm Life has been unique among life insurance companies in structuring shareholders' dividends. Stockholder dividends are limited to 10 percent of the original stock purchase price, or a maximum of $14,000 a year. All additional earnings must pay policyholder dividends or remain for the financial security of policyholders. The company paid almost $4 million in policyholder dividends in 2005. Since 1946, National Farm Life has

2005 President's Cabinet

Randy Robertson, Lubbock
Tory Henly, San Augustine
Don Bell, Palestine
Joe Harvick, Gainesville
Donnie Prater, Tulia
Donna CdeBaca, Lubbock
Shirley Clark, Amarillo
Doug Wall, Amarillo
Sam Lenoir, Groesbeck
Virginia Mendez, Amarillo
Frank McCullough, Pampa
John Harrell, Levelland
Paul Jones, Abilene
Edward Barela, Midland
Shere Forbes, Brownfield
Jerry Moosberg, Tyler
Nancy Smith, Hubbard
Russ Wright, Girard
Mark Hall, Hewitt
Sam White, Pampa
Donna Anderson, Hubbard
Craig Gehrels, CSA, Winters
Bobby Sisemore, LUTCF, Kress
Roy Chapman, Tyler
Joe Herring, Eastland
Mike A. Hill, Midland
Donna McGee, Lubbock
Eddie Tate Jr., Fort Worth
Steve Kosadnar, LUTCF, Athens
Tommy Hays, Fritch
Teressia Marley, Rotan
Cecil Glass, LUTCF, Waco
Gary Durham, Lubbock
Alicia Rodriguez, LUTCF, McAllen
Bill Schneider, Perryton

provided its policyholders with $59,931,268 in dividends and has paid more than $56 million in death benefits to beneficiaries.

National Farm Life is managed by President and CEO J. D. "Chip" Davis Jr. and Marketing Senior Vice President Cary L. Wright. Other vice presidents are Tom Buerk, Mark Bigsby, Sue Buerk, Linda Huens, Richard Jernigan, and Mark Williams. Collectively, these officers have amassed 195 years with National Farm Life. In the company's history, there have been only four presidents: Donald L. Jones Sr. (1946–1974), Donald L. Jones Jr. (1974–1999), Ronald G. Downing (1999–2004), and Chip Davis Jr. (2005–present).

National Farm Life has almost $2 billion of life insurance in force throughout Texas. The company has four state coordinators: Recruiting Director Monte Roach, from Lubbock; Area Coordinator Scott Anderson, from Hubbard; Area Coordinator Glen Baecker, CLU, from Goliad; and Area Coordinator Coy Worden, from Kaufman.

On March 10, 2006, National Farm Life celebrated its 60th year of providing for the financial needs of its policyholders through quality service from its agents and home office staff. The month-long celebration shattered all records for applications and premium production.

Success in the Community

In addition to its business successes, National Farm Life contributes significantly toward the stability of its community through a variety of activities and organizations. National Farm Life is involved in the Boy Scouts of America, the East Fort Worth Business Association, and the Fort Worth Adopt-A-School Program. The company also belongs to the industry's Texas Life Insurance Association, the American Council of Life Insurers, and IMSA (Insurance Marketplace Standards Association), whose goals are to strengthen trust and confidence in the life insurance industry and maintain standards of fairness, honesty, and openness in advertising, selling, and servicing clients. In 2000 National Farm Life formed the American Farm Life Insurance Company, which is licensed in Texas, Oklahoma, and New Mexico.

For 60 years National Farm Life has served the life insurance needs of Texas residents with integrity, efficiency, and economy. Its future success will stem from adhering to those same principles. National Farm Life Insurance Company has attained a position of prominence, not only in Fort Worth but also in the insurance industry.

Above: The members of National Farm Life Insurance Company's esteemed board of directors are, from left to right: (standing) Bob G. Walker, business development officer, Frost National Bank, Fort Worth; Philip E. Norwood, regional president for Tarrant County, Frost National Bank, Fort Worth; Ronald G. Downing, chairman, National Farm Life; Dr. John R. Abernathy, retired dean, College of Agricultural Sciences and Natural Resources, Texas Tech University; and J. D. "Chip" Davis Jr., president and CEO, National Farm Life; (seated) Dr. Leo Sayavedra, vice chancellor for academic and student affairs, Texas A & M University System; Dr. James G. Butler, deputy director general, Inter-American Institute for Cooperation in Agriculture; Paul Buchanan, CPA, attorney at law, Fort Worth; William M. Young, life underwriter and regional supervisor, National Farm Life; and Dr. Edward R. Nelson, physician, Fort Worth. Left: Just north of the main Dallas–Fort Worth highway, this distinctive building is one of the city's most notable landmarks.

wealth transfer, charitable giving, and more. The largest mutual fund company in the United States, Fidelity Investments continually improves its products, technology, and customer service.

Above: Fidelity Investments in Irving is one of the company's four Investor Centers in the Dallas–Fort Worth (DFW) area, which also include Dallas, Plano, and Southlake. Right: Fidelity established regional operations in the DFW area in 1983 and opened its Westlake regional headquarters, shown here, in 2001.

Fidelity Investments is one of the world's largest providers of financial services, offering investment management, retirement planning, brokerage, and human resources and benefits outsourcing services to more than 22 million individuals and institutions, as well as 5,500 financial intermediary firms.

Founded in Boston, Massachusetts, in 1946, Fidelity expanded to the Dallas–Fort Worth (DFW) area in 1983, its first expansion outside of Boston. Since then, the DFW Fidelity population has grown to 3,100 employees working at northeast Tarrant and Dallas County facilities in more than 20 Fidelity companies, with Investor Centers in Dallas, Irving, Plano, and Southlake. In addition, Fidelity has seven regional operations centers in the United States and Canada; several international offices, including locations in Hong Kong, Japan, France, India, Germany, Ireland, and the United Kingdom; and a total of 110 Investor Centers.

Fidelity is committed to supporting community and civic initiatives in northeast Texas. Fidelity employees contribute more than 5,000 hours annually, and the company supports many local organizations, including Carter BloodCare, the Amon Carter Museum, the American Heart Association, the North Texas and Tarrant Area Food Banks, Junior Achievement, the Carroll, Fort Worth, Keller, and Northwest Independent School Districts, and programs with Texas Christian University, the University of North Texas, and the University of Texas at Arlington.

As customers' needs have evolved, Fidelity has refined its existing offerings and developed new ones to meet those needs with a suite of lifetime solutions, including products for retirement rollover, retirement income and distribution, generational wealth transfer, college planning, life insurance, charitable giving, and others.

Since 1977, Fidelity has been led by Edward C. "Ned" Johnson III. Building upon the legacy of his father—the corporation's founder—Johnson has piloted Fidelity's growth from its early days as a U.S. mutual fund company to what is now a global financial services leader, the largest U.S. mutual fund company, the nation's number one provider of workplace retirement savings plans, a top-ranked discount broker, a preeminent provider of corporate benefits services, and one of the country's leading providers of investment products and services through financial intermediaries.

Fidelity's ability to adapt to changing market conditions for more than 60 years has been made possible by several company attributes that have remained unchanged since its inception: private ownership, continual improvement, a commitment to state-of-the-art technology, and superior customer service.

431990.1.0

Cash America International, Inc.

Serving America's 'underbanked,' this company helps hardworking people obtain money for life's cash emergencies. The first publicly owned pawnshop chain—and arguably the most successful, with 2005 revenues topping half a billion dollars—this Fort Worth company offers simple, accessible financial resources to its customers.

Cash America International, Inc. was founded in 1983 by Jack Daugherty, who began his career in the pawn business with a single pawnshop. Cash America is a provider of specialty financial services to individuals in more than 900 total locations and employs over 4,500 people across the United States. Daugherty continues to oversee the company as chairman of the board, and Dan Feehan is the company's president and CEO.

In 1987, the company made history by becoming the first chain of pawnshops to go public (its shares have been traded on the New York Stock Exchange since 1991, and are currently traded under the ticker symbol "CSH"). In 1988, Cash America opened its 100th pawnshop, and in 1992 its 200th shop opened.

In 2001, Cash America began offering short-term unsecured loans, better known as cash advances or payday loans, at many of its locations. By 2005, 464 Cash America pawnshops and 286 payday advance locations operated in 22 states. Today, Cash America is a market leader in small secured consumer pawn loans and small unsecured cash advance loans. Along the way to that distinction, Cash America added other services to its lending locations—check cashing, money orders, wire transfers, and stored value cards—with the goal of becoming the neighborhood financial services center. Cash America is committed to providing excellent customer service in a clean, professional setting.

Cash America's community service and close cooperation with local law enforcement are just two ways that the company is changing the perception of the pawn industry. The company has created innovative programs such as Keeping Communities Safe, Operation ID, and others to demonstrate that it is a responsible partner with the customers whose merchandise it handles.

Cash America is dedicated to the people who make up the "backbone of America." These hardworking people call on Cash America for short-term credit and other financial services. In 2005, Cash America facilitated almost $1.4 billion in consumer credit to its customers, making it a leader of small loans to individuals. Cash America International, Inc. is proud to be part of a way of life for many Americans and will continue to serve these customers.

Above: Cash America International, Inc.'s corporate headquarters is proudly located in Fort Worth, Texas.

has been closely restored to the original bank housed at the site in the early 1900s. Worthington National Bank offers full services, both traditional and on-line.

Clockwise from top left: The Worthington National Bank branch in Fort Worth has been carefully restored to its original architectural integrity and beauty. Attention to detail is evident in its exterior and interior, from its colonnaded facade to its marbled lobby (with artist Emily Guthrie Smith's *Branding Room* hanging on the left) to the handsome grillwork of its vault door.

With the motto "We don't close deals, we open relationships," Worthington National Bank puts a special emphasis on relationship-based banking. The bank has built its business one satisfied customer at a time, with the belief that if it takes care of its customers, the numbers will take care of themselves.

In addition, Worthington National Bank is extensively involved in its local communities. It regularly sponsors local charities, and its employees serve on numerous non-profit boards. Worthington National Bank also offers its boardroom and facilities for use by local and non-profit groups.

Almost all of Worthington National Bank's shareholders and employees are based in Tarrant County. Because the bank is locally owned, its profits and salaries recirculate within the local community and not on Wall Street.

Several of Worthington National Bank's locations are in historic buildings that have been carefully renovated and showcase artwork with many ties to the local community. These original pieces of Texas art accentuate the ambiance of this western-themed bank. The largest piece, *Branding Room*, was painted by Emily Guthrie Smith, who taught at Texas Christian University. The mural was salvaged from a fire at Fort Worth's now-razed Western Hills Hotel restaurant. Most of the remaining art in the bank's Sundance Square location was commissioned by Xiang Zhang. This Texas artist paints scenes primarily from the 6666 Ranch, which coincidentally was owned by Samuel "Burk" Burnett, after whom the bank's Fort Worth building is named.

Another benefit of Worthington National Bank is that there are no 800 telephone numbers, just a local 817 area code. The bank provides information about its services on its web site (www.worthingtonbank.com).

This big-city bank offers corporate and individual checking, savings, and money market accounts, and loans, with small-town customer service.

AmeriCredit

As a Fort Worth–based auto finance company with 2,000 Tarrant County employees, AmeriCredit connects customers with the vehicles they need. As a major employer and community partner, AmeriCredit contributes significantly to the communities in which its employees live and work.

Founded in 1992, AmeriCredit now serves more than one million customers in the United States and Canada. The company finances vehicles indirectly through automobile dealers as well as directly to consumers. Through its network of local sales representatives across North America, AmeriCredit maintains face-to-face relationships with more than 14,000 auto dealers. The company also has four collection centers, including its Arlington Operations Center in Arlington, Texas.

The company is a leader in the sub-prime auto finance industry, which includes customers with less-than-perfect credit histories. AmeriCredit also lends to customers with near-prime credit. And, in 2006, the company purchased Bay View Acceptance Corporation, whose customers have prime credit scores.

More than 4,000 employees in the United States and Canada have helped AmeriCredit expand its loan portfolio to $12 billion in managed auto receivables. This figure is expected to grow by an average of 10 percent to 15 percent each year.

Corporate Successes

High-profile magazines have recognized AmeriCredit (NYSE: ACF) for its financial accomplishments. In 2005, *Forbes* included the company among its 2,000 Largest Public Companies. That same year, AmeriCredit was also ranked in the Fortune 1,000 list of the biggest corporations, and in *Fortune*'s Diversified Financials industry category, AmeriCredit was ranked among the top 15, along with companies such as General Electric and American Express.

"We never set out to be the biggest," states Clifton H. Morris Jr., chairman of the board, who helped launch the company in 1992, "but we sure have worked hard to be the best at what we do. In my opinion, success is not necessarily guaranteed if you are the biggest. There is a strong possibility, however, that success will follow if you are the best."

Community Investments

In addition to investing in its own financial performance, AmeriCredit also gives money and time to more than 100 nonprofit organizations. The company concentrates most of its philanthropic work on United Way, the March of Dimes, and the Salvation Army. These national and international charities have locations near most of AmeriCredit's team members.

AmeriCredit's president and CEO Daniel E. Berce states, "Community investment has always been part of AmeriCredit's culture. We are very proud of our employees, who dedicate their time and energy to maximize the company's contributions to these worthwhile causes. AmeriCredit's future looks bright, so helping others is a natural way for us to share our success."

Above left: AmeriCredit, an industry-leading company, is guided by Clifton H. Morris Jr., chairman of the board (at left), and Daniel E. Berce, president and CEO. Above right: AmeriCredit is headquartered in Burnett Plaza in Fort Worth.

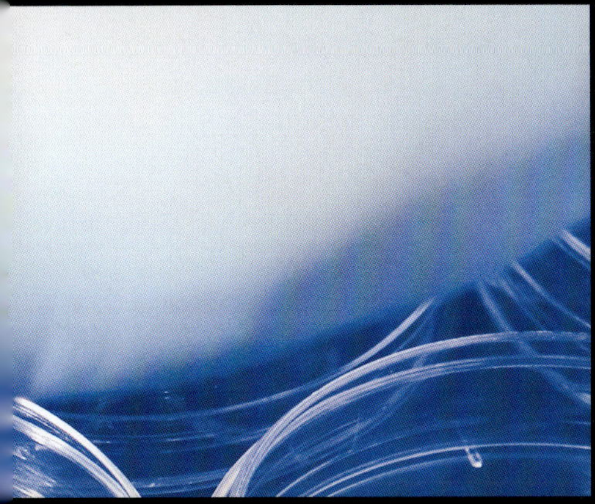

HEALTH CARE, PHARMACEUTICALS, AND BIOTECHNOLOGY
PROFILES OF COMPANIES AND ORGANIZATIONS

Cook Children's Health Care System

This pediatric health care delivery system is dedicated to preventing and treating illness and to improving the health of 'the Fort Worth area's most valuable resource, its children,' through hospitalization, outpatient services, and office visits.

Above: Cook Children's Medical Center in Fort Worth, Texas, is part of Cook Children's Health Care System, which also includes Cook Children's Physician Network, Cook Children's Home Health, Cook Children's Health Plan, and Cook Children's Health Foundation.

The mission of Cook Children's Health Care System is simple yet ambitious—to improve the health of every child in its region through the prevention and treatment of illness, disease, and injury.

Children's health has been a priority in the Fort Worth community since early in the 20th century. In fact, Cook Children's dates back to the Fort Worth Free Baby Hospital, which opened its doors in 1918 under the leadership of Ida L. Turner, a former postmistress. Then in 1929, W. I. Cook Memorial Hospital was opened, with 55 beds. The facility was endowed by Matilda Cook, of the Cook Ranch in Albany, Texas, and named in memory of her late husband and daughter. However, during the polio epidemic in the 1950s, the hospital's board of trustees voted to expand the facility and change its mission to care exclusively for children. It was renamed Cook Children's Hospital. In 1961, the Fort Worth Free Baby Hospital was relocated in a new facility, and the hospital was renamed Fort Worth Children's Hospital. The two children's hospitals merged in 1985, and the new Cook Children's Medical Center was opened in 1989.

In 1995, the trustees officially changed the name to Cook Children's Medical Center and formed Cook Children's Health Care System.

In addition to the medical center, the health care system includes Cook Children's Physician Network, Cook Children's Home Health, Cook Children's Health Plan, and a fund-raising organization, Cook Children's Health Foundation.

A Vital System

Today, Cook Children's touches the lives of nearly one million patients annually—through hospitalization, outpatient services, and office visits. Each year, more than 400,000 children visit a pediatric office within the system; 85,000 are treated in the emergency room; 43,000 are treated at the health care system's urgent care centers; some 10,000 children are admitted to the medical center; more than 16,000 undergo surgical procedures; and more than 1,000 receive home health care. These patients come from 120 counties in Texas, 35 other states, and various foreign countries.

In light of such statistics, it is not surprising that Cook Children's Health Care System, with more than 3,800 employees, is among the leading employers in Tarrant County.

Child-Friendly

Cook Children's is organized to deliver patient-centered care. Well positioned to meet the specific medical and physical needs of newborns, children, and adolescents, Cook Children's Medical Center has more than 500 affiliated physicians, offering pediatric care in more than

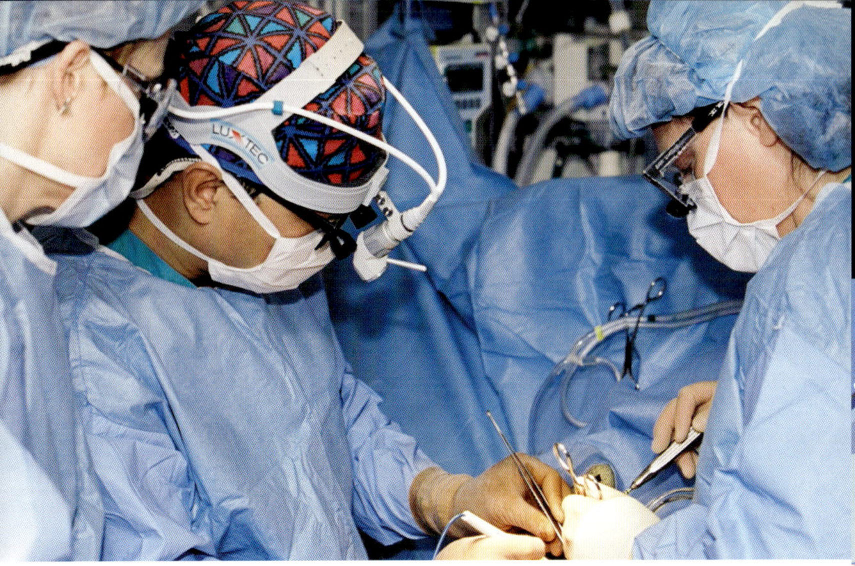

30 specialties. The medical center is furnished with child-appropriate facilities and features, such as playrooms with aquariums, video games, and computers.

Cook Children's is nationally recognized for several of its specialties, including cardiology and cardiothoracic surgery, hematology/oncology, critical care, neurology and neurosurgery, and pulmonology.

Cook Children's Heart Center, which was expanded in 2005, offers comprehensive diagnostics and treatments for most congenital heart defects and diseases. In 2000, it was the first pediatric facility in the United States with the EnSite3000 cardiac mapping system, allowing cardiologists better and faster pinpointing of abnormal rhythms. Three years later it became the first pediatric facility in the nation to use cryoablation to correct arrhythmia.

Cook Children's Hematology and Oncology Center specializes in childhood cancers and blood disorders such as hemophilia, sickle cell anemia, and genetic abnormalities.

Cook Children's Bone Marrow and Stem Cell Transplantation service—which is affiliated with the National Marrow Donor Program as a donor registry, donor collection, and transplant center—is a national leader in the use of bone marrow transplants for nonmalignant blood disorders. As of January 2006, the program had completed more than 600 bone marrow/stem cell transplants.

Cook Children's also has the only pediatric trauma center in Tarrant County, Texas, and sees more than 85,000 children annually. In addition to emergency and trauma care, the medical center also offers newborn intensive care (NICU), pediatric intensive care (PICU), and extracorporeal membrane oxygenation (ECMO). Its pediatric transport services carry more than 1,800 critical care children annually by ambulance, helicopter, and the Teddy Bear Transport airplane, which is fully equipped and is staffed with critical care nurses and technicians.

The Cook Children's Neuroscience Center has one of the largest pediatric neuroscience programs in the Southwest. The center offers comprehensive services, including neurosurgery, neurorehabilitation, epilepsy monitoring units, and neuropsychology and radiology services. Expanded neurology and neurosurgery facilities include an intraoperative neuroimaging (iMRI) center.

The dedicated Cook Children's staff is specially trained in child development. Staff members not only provide high quality medical care, but also offer compassionate support to patients and their families. The staff is available to assist families with stress associated with children's illnesses or injuries.

As an advocate for children, Cook Children's often goes beyond its walls to collaborate with other organizations within the community to help children become productive adults.

Prognosis for the Future

The health care system's strategic plan, Every Child 2020, challenges the system to deliver patient-centered clinical care while supporting its values of safety, caring, innovation, collaboration, integrity, and giving.

Each year, Cook Children's provides more than $175 million in uncompensated care to uninsured and underinsured children. Cook Children's Health Foundation provides numerous options to help these patients and support the needs of a growing population.

Russell K. Tolman, president and CEO of Cook Children's Health Care System, says, "Our vision is to provide quality health care to ill and injured children. Our efforts, along with the generous donations received by our foundation, are truly an investment in the future of the community."

Cook Children's Medical Center has more than 500 affiliated physicians. Above left: Vincent K. Tam, M.D., specializes in cardiothoracic surgery, general surgery, and surgical critical care. Above right: Gretchen M. Eames, M.D., specializes in pediatric hematology and oncology.

Built on the innovative idea of two Fort Worth pharmacists to make sterile eye products, this global company is the world leader in ophthalmic pharmaceutical, surgical, and consumer products, with 13,000 employees in more than 75 countries and distribution in more than 180 countries.

Above: Alcon, Inc. broke ground on its Fort Worth campus in 1958, building a manufacturing facility, laboratory, and administration building on a 175-acre site south of town. Today the facility encompasses dozens of administrative, research, and production buildings. Right: Alcon's first location, a retail pharmacy, opened in 1945 in downtown Fort Worth. To accommodate the store's growing clientele, Alcon's founders, Bob Alexander and Bill Conner, added two drive-up windows.

In 1945 two Fort Worth pharmacists had a simple idea: make sterile eye products and sell them to local physicians. The small enterprise Bill Conner and Bob Alexander created eventually became Alcon, Inc., the worldwide leader in ophthalmic pharmaceutical, surgical, and consumer products by market share, with annual sales approaching $5 billion in 2006.

Alcon is now a research and development-driven medical specialty company focused on eye care. The company develops, manufactures, and markets the broadest product portfolio of ophthalmic pharmaceuticals, surgical equipment and devices, and consumer eye care products in the ophthalmic industry.

Alcon has 13,000 people working in more than 75 countries, and it sells its products in more than 180 countries. About half of its employees are in the United States, with about 3,000 working at the company's U.S. headquarters in Fort Worth.

This global business started as a modest pharmacy. Founders Bill Conner and Bob Alexander combined the first syllables of their last names to create the name "Alcon." Former CEO Tim Sear jokes that it was a good thing the men decided to merge their last names instead of their first, or the company might be confused with Billy Bob's, the legendary Fort Worth honky-tonk.

As a sideline to the pharmacy, Conner and Alexander also compounded sterile ophthalmic products—products not otherwise available at the time—for doctors. After experiencing initial success in this effort, they eventually closed the pharmacy and devoted themselves exclusively to manufacturing and promoting eye care products for ophthalmologists. Their plan was soon tested when the Trinity River flooded in 1949 and destroyed their facilities. Undaunted, they sought higher ground for a new campus and acquired 175 acres at Alcon's present location,

southeast of the intersection of Interstates 20 and 35.

In 1972, with sales of only about $40 million, Alcon became a publicly traded company for the first time by listing its shares on the New York Stock Exchange. In the next five years, Alcon's sales nearly doubled, making it an attractive acquisition for a larger company—Nestlé, S.A., the world's largest food company—which was looking for new avenues of growth. For the next 25 years, Alcon operated as a unit of Nestlé.

Under then-CEO Ed Schollmaier, Alcon worked to become the undisputed leader in its market. It increased its research facilities and spending and built or expanded its manufacturing and distribution facilities around the world. In 1989, Alcon bought the leading ophthalmic surgical company at the time, CooperVision Surgical, which now accounts for almost half of Alcon's sales. By 2001, Alcon was the clear leader in ophthalmology products, with sales of $2.75 billion.

In 2002, Alcon re-emerged as a publicly traded company (NYSE: ACL) when Nestlé sold 25 percent of its shares. Alcon's was the largest health care initial public offering (IPO) at the time of the IPO, at just more than $2.5 billion in proceeds, reflecting a total market capitalization of $10 billion. Over the next three years, sales again nearly doubled, and today Alcon, at more than $30 billion, has the largest market capitalization of any public company in Tarrant County.

Alcon is also deeply committed to humanitarian efforts and community involvement. The company and its employees are among the largest contributors in the area to United Way and Junior Achievement, and Alcon actively supports Habitat for Humanity, the Salvation Army, Tarrant Area Food Bank, and other organizations. Alcon annually opens its campus to more than 2,000 people for a walk-athon to benefit Prevent Blindness Texas, helping its local chapter raise more money to reduce blindness than any other chapter of Prevent Blindness America. The company annually sponsors more than 1,000 medical missions to less-developed countries to help restore sight to those without access to eye care. Since Alcon's IPO, its annual global humanitarian contributions have more than doubled, reaching $48 million in 2005.

While the company's founders may not have fully imagined the possibilities, their forward-thinking approach created a formula for success that guides Alcon today. Under the leadership of Cary Rayment, chairman, president, and CEO, Alcon is pursuing its vision of being the first choice for eye care products around the world and plans to be the eye care industry leader for many years to come.

Above: By the early 1960s, Alcon's production line included custom-designed machinery that could automatically fill, plug, cap, and seal the company's unique plastic Drop-Tainer dispenser bottles, which became a pharmaceutical industry standard after their invention in Fort Worth. Left: Today the Alcon campus houses some of the world's most advanced ophthalmic research and production facilities, including a manufacturing plant that produces products used by both consumers and physicians.

are pushing back the frontiers of their respective fields, making remarkable advances in super-subspecialty medicine.

Above: True to the spirit of its beloved city and state, Plaza Medical Center of Fort Worth does not "fence itself in," choosing instead to pursue progress along several frontiers at once. By providing a broad range of "wellness care" services, in addition to diagnosis and treatment by professionals using the most advanced methods, Plaza contributes to the overall health of the community and helps maintain the superb quality of life in North Texas.

Plaza Medical Center of Fort Worth is where the frontiers of life and medicine meet:

- the great cattle drives along the legendary Chisholm Trail
- the ranching-family matriarch, whose heart skips a beat when she lifts her granddaughter out of the car safety seat
- the pink-granite courthouse high on the bluffs above the river
- railcars converging from every point on the compass
- the oilfield roughneck with the arthritic hip
- "Rosie the Riveter" and her sisters assembling the arsenal of freedom out at the "bomber plant"
- the PGA golfer with the aching back ambling down the 18th fairway at Colonial, hoping to be fitted for a plaid jacket one more time

Plaza Medical Center of Fort Worth has never focused on just one frontier at a time. From its home at the crossroads of the city's Medical District, it offers a broad range of services spanning key disciplines such as cardiology, neurology, oncology, and orthopedics, as well as several types of super-subspecialty surgery.

Plaza takes pride in serving as a major referral center for complex and difficult cases from all over Tarrant County and the communities to the west. It has twice received national recognition from Solucient as a Top 100 Heart Hospital, and its heart attack–treatment program is one of only a handful across the nation to have been certified by the Joint Committee on the Accreditation of Healthcare Organizations. The Texas Nurses Association includes Plaza among an elite group of hospitals it designates as "nurse-friendly," signifying it finds Plaza an ideal environment for the practice of nursing.

Excellence in the Art and Science of Health Care

A $90 million Plaza expansion and renovation project has added

more than 30,000 square feet of new space and has also brought some 40,000 square feet of major improvements to existing facilities such as operating rooms, the surgery waiting area, and the critical care unit.

An additional 25,000 square feet of space within the hospital has been completely updated with new decor and furnishings. This undertaking extended to the remodeling of every patient room and nurses' station.

Each year, Plaza is caring for more and more patients in its primary service area, a testament to its stature in the community and region:

- Overall admissions have been growing at a rate between 5 and 10 percent annually.
- Outpatient visits consistently outpace those of the previous year by double-digit margins.
- Year-over-year increases in the number of surgical procedures performed have exceeded 25 percent.
- When it comes to patient satisfaction, Plaza is in the top 10 percent (and climbing) of the nearly 200 hospitals nationwide owned and operated by the Hospital Corporation of America (HCA Inc.).

Plaza is also recording all-time high scores on surveys measuring physician and nurse satisfaction, is contributing more time and money to community and charitable organizations, and is logging continual improvement on all important measurements of performance and quality.

It all comes down to this: when surgeons perform a super-subspecialty procedure requiring tremendous skill and technical know-how, they are actually focusing on something else—getting the patient back to life.

That is why, when Plaza Medical Center talks about the advances in its own world, it is also talking about advances in the patient's world—even if that just means being able to sit pain-free and carefree on the front porch on a summer evening, sipping a cool drink and listening to the song of the cicadas.

At Plaza Medical Center of Fort Worth, it is that simple—"We do difficult. You do life."

Above right and left: The physicians, nurses, administrators, and support personnel at Plaza Medical Center of Fort Worth share the dreams and aspirations of their fellow North Texans. Thanks to them, Plaza has grown and developed at a pace mirroring that of Fort Worth itself. That is why North Texans from all walks of life—cowboys and corporate executives, airline pilots and police officers—count on Plaza for top-notch medical care delivered with compassion and wisdom.

pharmaceuticals, over-the-counter drugs, and other medical supplies through its many affiliates. It has become a global leader in the tissue management, dermatology, and surgical antiseptic markets.

Above: DFB Pharmaceuticals, Inc. shares headquarters with affiliates Healthpoint, Ltd. and Coria Laboratories, Ltd.

DFB Pharmaceuticals, Inc. is making its mark on the local Fort Worth business landscape and on the pharmaceutical industry worldwide. A fully integrated pharmaceutical company, DFB supplies outstanding research and manufacturing services, branded pharmaceutical products, and innovative technologies to the global health care marketplace.

Just halfway into its second decade, the company has grown from annual sales of $21 million in 1991 to more than $353 million in 2005. Nurtured by Fort Worth's business climate, the organization and its operating companies anticipate continued expansion of its key business segments nationally and internationally.

DFB's success has been propelled by synergistic relationships with affiliates Healthpoint®, Ltd.; Coria™ Laboratories, Ltd.; DPT Laboratories®, Ltd.; DFB Bioscience; DFB Biotech, Inc.; and Phyton Biotech, Inc.

Healthpoint®, Ltd.; Coria™ Laboratories, Ltd.

Sharing headquarters with DFB in west Fort Worth is Healthpoint, a company founded by DFB in 1992 to focus on the research, development, and marketing of branded pharmaceuticals, over-the-counter drugs, and medical devices. The impressive DFB-Healthpoint campus stretches from the Hulen and West Vickery intersection for nearly a half-mile west to the building at 4900 West Vickery Boulevard. The campus is a major landmark situated less than a mile south of Interstate 30 in an active corridor for health care, business, banking, education, and retail.

Healthpoint's business reach is local, national, and global. Its technology-driven products impact doctors, hospitals, group-purchasing organizations, and licensing partners in 14 countries. Professionals use Healthpoint's patented products for tissue management, dermatology, and surgical indications related to the treatment and prevention of diseased and traumatized skin and soft tissues as well as the treatment and prevention of infection.

A leading pharmaceutical wound and skin care company, Healthpoint has five preeminent brands in its wound care portfolio: Accuzyme®, Panafil®, Xenaderm®, Santyl®, and Oasis®, all marketed under the aegis of Healthpoint Tissue Management.

Healthpoint's dermatology division, Coria Laboratories, specializes in products for the treatment of diseases affecting the skin, hair, and nails. Coria's most recent brand introductions include Salex™ in 2004 and CeraVe™ in 2005.

Healthpoint Surgical is represented in hundreds of hospital operating rooms by the innovative Trizenol™ product line that includes Triseptin®, the first in a Healthpoint-created category called "brush-free surgical scrubs."

Internationally, Healthpoint has business relationships in North America, Central America, Europe, North Africa, Southeast Asia, and Australia.

Phyton Biotech, Inc.

Also on the global map is DFB affiliate Phyton Biotech, Inc., which develops and utilizes proprietary plant cell culture technology at its facilities in Princeton, New Jersey, and in Ahrensburg, Germany.

DFB Bioscience; DFB Biotech, Inc.

Rounding out the growing family of companies are DFB Bioscience, a cell-based therapeutic research and development group in Lausanne, Switzerland, and DFB Biotech, Inc. of Curaçao, Netherlands Antilles, each acquired in 2005 and 2006, respectively. These two enterprises focus on biological therapeutics. Biopharmaceutical enterprises combine the best of biological forms found naturally in humans, animals, and plants with chemically derived products known as pharmaceuticals.

DPT Laboratories®, Ltd.

Many DFB products, biologics, and technologies are produced by affiliate DPT Laboratories, Ltd., a contract development and manufacturing organization serving the pharmaceutical industry worldwide. DPT has facilities in Texas and New Jersey, but its reach is global. Its customers include many of the world's top 50 pharmaceutical and consumer products companies. DPT is widely recognized as the industry choice for semisolid and liquid development, manufacturing, and packaging services for pharmaceutical, biotechnology, and health care companies. DPT is also known for other more complex drug-delivery forms.

Texas Roots

DFB's origins date back to 1938 and the Texas Pharmacal Company (TPC), used by Warner-Lambert (W-L) to manufacture Lubriderm® and other W-L products. In 1966 W-L acquired TPC, then sold it to Alcon Laboratories, Inc. in 1979. Alcon renamed the company Dermatological Products of Texas (now DPT Laboratories). DFB purchased DPT from Alcon in 1990.

DFB formed its affiliates to develop and market unique health care–related products and leverage DPT's technical capabilities.

Through years of steady growth, acquisition, and expansion, DFB and its affiliates honor their heritage. DFB has 1,800 employees globally and more than 250 in the Dallas–Fort Worth area. At its Fort Worth campus, DFB will complete Building Four, a 78,000-square-foot research and development facility, in the first quarter of 2007. As of 2006, DFB has brought 15 patented products to the professional health care market, confirming Fort Worth's position as a platform for health care–related enterprises. The spotlight on DFB Pharmaceuticals' development of innovative new products and technologies will only intensify in the future.

Above left: DFB's scientists develop innovative technologies and products. Above right: Phyton Biotech utilizes cutting-edge plant cell fermentation technology.

This longtime Fort Worth health care provider strives to provide exemplary care for the community at every opportunity—from preventive medicine to advanced treatment methods for fighting disease—focusing on patient care, education, research, and community service.

Since its founding in 1906, Baylor All Saints Medical Center at Fort Worth has provided advanced health care to its community. Located near downtown Fort Worth, the center began as All Saints Episcopal Hospital, which cared for the sick on the Texas frontier. It grew steadily during the first half of the century, becoming a progressive health center devoted to quality medical care, public health education, research, and community service.

Over the decades, Baylor All Saints at Fort Worth continued to offer leading-edge health care and opened specialized medical centers such as the Moncrief Cancer Center, the Moncrief Ambulatory Care Center, and the Carter Rehabilitation & Fitness Center.

A Second Hospital

In 1987, Baylor All Saints at Fort Worth built a second full-service hospital—All Saints Hospital Cityview, today named Baylor Medical Center at Southwest Fort Worth. At this facility, the people of southwest Tarrant County can receive quality general acute care and obstetrical, gynecological, and emergency services. In addition, specialty physicians are available in the center's medical office buildings.

Above right: A new day dawns for Baylor All Saints Medical Center at Fort Worth, the founding hospital of Baylor All Saints Medical Centers, where world-class medicine, physicians, and patient care intersect.

Neuroscience Center

In 2001, Baylor All Saints at Fort Worth opened the Laura Leonard Hallum Neuroscience Center, which offers advances such as Gamma Knife[1] deep brain stimulation, neck and spine surgical services, and a stroke program.

Expanded Resources

In 2002, All Saints Hospitals formed an affiliation with the Baylor Health Care System (BHCS), a not-for-profit, faith-based network of hospitals, primary care centers, rehabilitation clinics, senior health centers, affiliated ambulatory surgery centers, and the Baylor Research Institute. With the affiliation, the two hospitals were renamed Baylor All Saints Medical Center at Fort Worth and Baylor Medical Center at Southwest Fort Worth, together forming Baylor All Saints Medical Centers. The affiliation also brought access to the resources of BHCS. One result is a partnership of Baylor Regional Transplant Institute with Baylor All Saints Medical Center at Fort Worth, which opened an inpatient transplant unit. Expansion at Baylor All Saints Medical Center at Fort Worth continues, including the new Andrews Women's Hospital, which is projected for completion in 2008.

Today, Baylor All Saints Medical Centers continues to excel in all its health care services, including cancer care, transplants, neurosciences, rehabilitation, cardiovascular care, women's services, and more. It is committed to providing quality health care that makes a difference in the lives of people in greater Fort Worth.

[1]Gamma Knife is owned by and leased from an affiliate of HealthSouth and is a service of Baylor All Saints Medical Center. The Gamma Knife is not a joint venture of HealthSouth and Baylor All Saints Medical Center. The physicians providing Gamma Knife services are independent physicians.

Neurological Services of Texas, P.A.

For more than 30 years, this Fort Worth neurology practice has provided compassionate, superior care—from diagnosing disorders to treating them—to patients in the area. Founder Susan Blue, M.D., has taken prominent leadership roles in her field and in the civic life of the city.

Neurological Services of Texas, P.A. and its founder, Susan Blue, M.D., have been in the Fort Worth medical community for more than 30 years. When Blue came to Fort Worth in 1973, for five years she was one of only two neurologists in the area. She set a high standard for neurological care that continues today. Her first priority has always been her patients; her chief concern is their evaluation and care.

Today, Neurological Services of Texas is a thriving clinical practice that provides neurological evaluation, diagnostic procedures, and treatment for patients of age 16 and above. The clinic evaluates and treats disorders such as multiple sclerosis, Alzheimer's disease and other forms of dementia, stroke, Parkinson's disease, seizures, headaches, and dizziness. It diagnoses patients using procedures such as electroencephalography, or brain-wave testing (EEG), to evaluate dizziness, blackouts, and seizures. It also uses electromyography (EMG) and nerve conduction velocity testing (NCV) to evaluate neck and back pain, numbness, and a spectrum of neurological symptoms.

Impeccable Credentials, Community Leadership

Often described as a "Renaissance woman," Blue graduated Phi Beta Kappa in mathematics from Randolph-Macon Woman's College in Virginia. She then earned her M.D. and completed a fellowship in cerebrovascular disease from Wake Forest University School of Medicine in Winston-Salem, North Carolina.

Blue is strongly committed to Fort Worth and to the medical community. A member of the Medical Advisory Board of the State of Texas, Blue has served as president of the Tarrant County Medical Society and the Texas Neurological Society. She also was a gubernatorial appointee to the Rehabilitation Council of Texas.

Within her community, Blue is a board member of the Fort Worth Chamber of Commerce, and she has held leadership positions in Bridge Emergency Youth Services, the Circle Theatre Board, and The Women's Center of Tarrant County.

Reflections on Neurology

In the 30 years that Blue has practiced medicine, the field of neurology has advanced significantly. Calling these changes "very exciting," Blue adds, "We are able to treat people for things we never even had a chance to diagnose before. However, in the midst of all these advancements, we must strive to provide the individual care needed by patients and coordinate that care management with the other providers involved. It all comes down to a coordinated continuity of care. That will be our next challenge."

Above: Susan Blue, M.D., began Neurological Services of Texas, P.A. in 1973.

Committed to helping people find a better way to fully experience life, this medical institute combines years of worldwide research with a new branch of medicine to revitalize patients. Its programs of preventive medicine, nutrition, supplementation, fitness training, and aesthetic procedures are designed to improve overall well-being.

IAM

The Institute of Age Management and Aesthetic Medicine

Above: The Institute of Age Management and Aesthetic Medicine strives to return a person to his or her younger self, allowing the individual to regain focus, energy, sex drive, clarity, and stamina. The institute uses preventive medicine, combined with a low-glycemic diet, cardiovascular and resistance training, vitamin and nutritional regimens, and bioidentical hormonal supplementation, to help patients restore vitality lost to the aging process.

Everyone wants to look and feel their best at every age. At the Institute of Age Management and Aesthetic Medicine (IAM) in Fort Worth, physicians trained in this medical subspecialty assist patients in their personal journey toward total well-being, inside and out. The institute's two-pronged approach combines age management medicine and aesthetic medicine to help individuals reclaim their energy, become mentally sharp and physically fit, increase disease resistance, and look their best.

Age management medicine—the first half of the equation—includes a series of precise tests to help determine a person's biological age. By testing various chemicals and hormonal levels in the blood, medical professionals can determine and compare a person's chronological age with his or her biological age. Energy-expenditure mapping; whole body composition; bone density scans; electrocardiograms; blood tests, such as intracellular nutritional assays; and other analytical processes draw a picture of the inner age of the body.

Using the information obtained, hormones or nutrients that are found to be deficient in the patient are replaced using supplements, nutrition, and fitness regimens. Each program is physician directed and patient specific in its design to help restore the body to a higher level of youthfulness, enabling patients to renew and regain their mental clarity, energy, sex drive, and stamina. This approach is only half of the institute's strategy for producing enhanced vigor, increased self-confidence, and a life that can be lived to the fullest.

The second half of the program is accomplished through aesthetic medicine, which matches a patient's outward appearance with the renewed, more youthful inner self. Most procedures are simple and can be completed in the state-of-the-art IAM outpatient clinic. Aesthetic medicine combines various therapies to improve the patient's physical appearance. Mesotherapy, minimally invasive "thread" face-lift, photodynamic therapy, laser resurfacing, reduction of unwanted hair, and vein treatment are just some of the techniques that enable people to look as good as they feel.

Aesthetic medicine includes high quality, pharmaceutical-grade cosmetics known as "cosmeceuticals." IAM offers four lines that it considers to be among the finest available—Obagi, Jan Marini, Procyte, and ColoreScience. IAM physicians know how to tailor a regimen for each patient's therapy and post-treatment needs.

Once people come to the realization that they can do something about the effects of aging, the institute helps them achieve results that go beyond simply looking young. It can help individuals reclaim the well-being and health—inside and out—that enables them to enjoy life and achieve their personal best at any age.

Harris Methodist Fort Worth Hospital

Serving Tarrant County since 1930, this outstanding hospital has earned many high honors, including a spot on Solucient's list of '100 Top Hospitals' for six consecutive years and the distinction of being voted the 'Best Place to Have a Baby' by *Fort Worth Child* magazine every year since 1993.

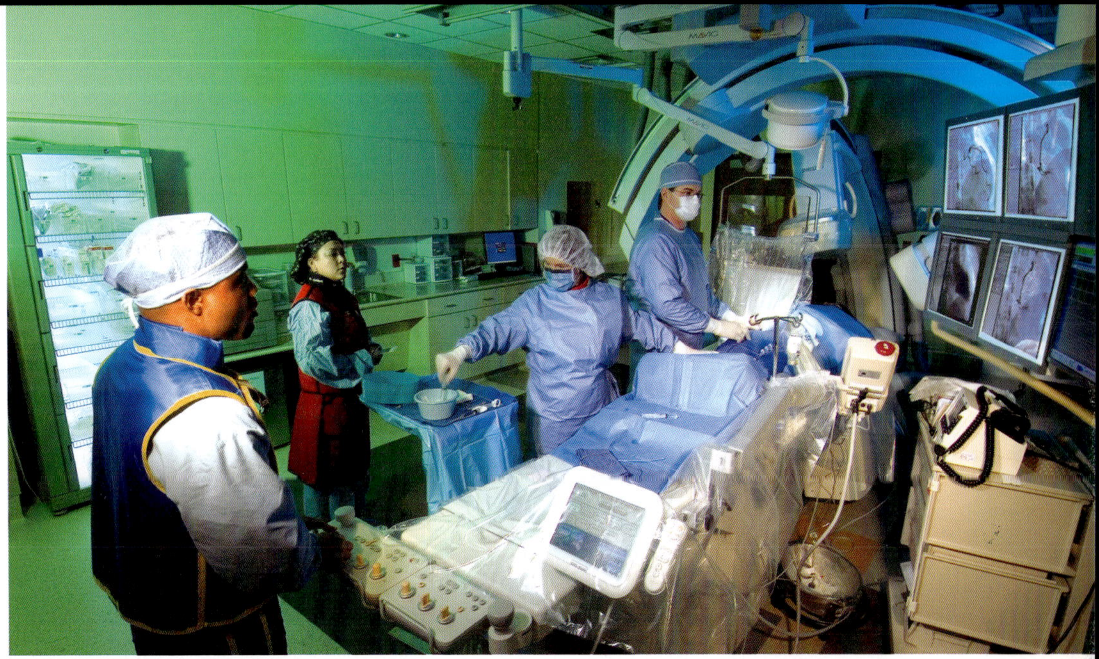

Committed to high quality patient care and the most advanced medical procedures, Harris Methodist Fort Worth Hospital (HMFW) specializes in oncology, trauma treatment, cardiology, and women's services, just to name a few of this hospital's multiple specialties. As the flagship facility of Harris Methodist Hospitals, HMFW also offers a broad range of services for every stage of life, constantly renovating departments and adding services based on the community's needs.

In 2006 the Harris Methodist Heart Center was opened. This 150,000-square-foot, $62 million facility houses 100 dedicated cardiac beds, four interventional laboratories, and four surgery suites dedicated to cardiac procedures. In the same year, the hospital completed its first stage of renovating the mother/baby suites, creating a homelike environment for new families. Women & Infants' Health Services offers a Level III neonatal intensive care unit and an Antenatal Assessment Center, and is the area's leading perinatal referral center for high-risk obstetrics.

The hospital's neurosciences and cancer services department also features such advanced technology as the CyberKnife® Stereotactic Radiosurgery system, which offers treatment for tumors that were once considered inoperable. This innovative surgery is incision-free and painless, and delivers radiation doses with pinpoint accuracy to prevent damage to healthy tissue.

Other special programs include Assisted Reproductive Technology Services, offering a full range of services focused on infertility treatment and in vitro fertilization, and the Healing Arts Center, providing complementary therapy from certified professionals in the areas of aromatherapy, massage, and reflexology. Treatment for sports injuries is available at the Ben Hogan Sports Therapy Institute, where professional, collegiate, high school, and amateur athletes receive athletic training, massage therapy, sports physical therapy, and performance conditioning.

Committed to personalized service since its inception, HMFW was founded after Dr. Charles H. Harris suggested that the Methodist Church build a hospital in Fort Worth. The hospital was opened in 1930. During the next 75 years, HMFW expanded to meet the needs of the community, keeping a patient-oriented philosophy at the center of its mission while offering the most advanced medical treatment and technology available. Today, the 710-bed hospital and Level II trauma center has a medical staff of nearly 1,000 physicians.

HMFW was the first and is currently the only adult hospital in Tarrant County to receive the Magnet Recognition Program® Award. This award, conferred by the American Nurses Association, means patients can expect quality care and attention from a qualified and award-winning nursing staff.

Harris Methodist Fort Worth Hospital is proud of its Fort Worth heritage and looks forward to another 75 years of caring for the community.

HARRIS METHODIST
Fort Worth Hospital
Texas Health Resources

Above: Harris Methodist Fort Worth Hospital has been a community partner continually providing quality, technologically advanced health care options for the residents of Tarrant County since opening its doors in 1930. Its Heart Center, which opened in January 2006, provides leading-edge medical technology throughout and includes four cardiac catheterization laboratories.

INDUSTRIAL GOODS AND SERVICES
PROFILES OF COMPANIES AND ORGANIZATIONS

For more than a quarter of a century, this Fort Worth company has been known for its unwavering commitment to excellence in customer service. Built with ingenuity and dedication, this leading machinery-moving, rigging, millwright, and installation contractor offers a diverse range of quality services.

Above left: Joanne and Neal Ingle, founders and owners of DFW Movers & Erectors, Inc., believe, "We could move the whole world if we had a place to put it." Whether moving single machines or an entire operational facility, DFW Movers is truly focused on satisfying its customers—from assessing the turnkey requirements and scope of each project to the final details of equipment installation. Above right: Crate Master, a division of DFW Movers, can handle and crate everything from heavy industrial equipment to a client's finest antiques. Here equipment is prepared with a barrier bag and banding for shipment. Below right: Two 40,000- to 60,000-pound capacity forklifts with booms are used to move a press brake.

Joanne and Neal Ingle founded DFW Movers & Erectors, Inc. in 1980 with one truck and a commitment to quality service and customer satisfaction. Their mission was to provide trained personnel, specialized equipment, and professional rigging and millwright services for the installation and relocation of industrial equipment.

Joanne Ingle, chief executive officer and president, elaborates. "Our ultimate goal is to please the customer. We don't cut corners, and we stand by our work," she says.

When the company was founded, Neal delivered equipment, installed machines, and operated hydraulic tilt-bed trucks while Joanne was the dispatcher, the job scheduler, and the accounting manager. Today, this Fort Worth–based company is one of the leading rigging and millwright contractors in the nation.

'One Machine or a Complete Plant'

DFW Movers' slogan, "One machine or a complete plant," reflects the diversity of the services it offers. A member of the Specialized Carriers and Rigging Association (SC&RA) for more than 25 years, DFW Movers has the proficiency and state-of-the-art technology to move a single machine or relocate an entire facility.

No item is too heavy or too delicate for DFW Movers. The company is equipped to move/relocate everything from food processing and metal stamping equipment to magnetic resonance imaging (MRI) machines and fragile sculptures. This versatility helps DFW Movers serve clients in a wide range of industries, including aerospace, automotive, energy, food and beverage, high-tech, mechanical contracting, medical, and cleanroom services.

More than Just Movers

DFW Movers, however, is not just a machinery-moving company. As the business has grown, it has expanded its services to meet customers' needs and expectations. In 1996, DFW Movers formed Crate Master, a separate division for fabricating crates for local or overseas containers.

Today, Crate Master designs and builds custom crates for large items such as airplanes, helicopters, automobiles, and mail sorting equipment as well as for smaller items such as chandeliers, paintings, and antiques.

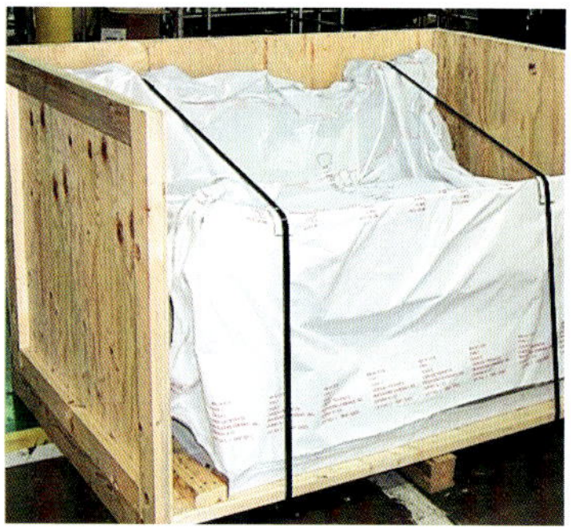

Crate Master can provide in-house or on-site crating and uncrating, both locally and nationwide. It can also arrange for domestic or international shipping. From wood boxes and pallet boxes to helicopter pallets, shock-absorbing skids, and vapor barrier bags, Crate Master can accommodate virtually any crating need. DFW Movers can also provide warehousing to store equipment on either a temporary or long-term basis.

DFW Movers' Laser Precision Division fills another of its customers' needs—aligning and calibrating machine tools. The division's employees are factory-trained as laser precision specialists and use Hamar Laser, Renishaw, Ballbar, and Lasermike alignment systems. They can diagnose critical machinery and then align and restore the equipment to precision accuracy, optimum productivity, and quality standards.

In addition to these services, DFW Movers provides retrofitting and repair. Its Expert millwrights are capable of quick repairs as well as rebuilding or remanufacturing to ensure that customers' equipment operates efficiently and effectively. As a finishing touch, DFW Movers can make old machinery look new with fast, cost-efficient electrostatic painting.

DFW Movers expanded in 2002 and opened an additional location in San Marcos, Texas. Outgrowing the San Marcos facility quickly, the company then moved those operations to Kyle, Texas, located between Austin and San Antonio. DFW Kyle offers the same services as its home office in Fort Worth: machinery moving, rigging, crating, laser services, warehousing, electrostatic painting, clean room services, and retrofitting.

Beyond the Move

Both Joanne and Neal Ingle are quick to point out that even with state-of-the-art equipment, employees are the company's most important asset. In fact, DFW Movers has minimal turnover among its employees, many of whom have been with the company for more than 10 years.

"Our success is a blessing," Joanne says. "We care about our employees and our customers. We believe that when we receive something good, it is important to give back and lend a hand."

To that end, Joanne serves on several boards and is involved in various business and charitable organizations, including Race for the Cure, Smiling Women's Project, Toys for Tots, Women's Haven Shelter, and the March of Dimes.

Additionally, DFW Movers is an active member of the Fort Worth, Dallas, San Antonio, San Marcos, and U.S. chambers of commerce.

As a company that stands by its work, its employees, its customers, and its community, DFW Movers is certain to keep on moving into the 21st century with the same commitment to service and quality it envisioned when it was founded more than two decades ago.

Above left: DFW Movers provides clean room services including equipment installation. Above right: A DFW Movers employee operates a 400-ton hydraulic gantry to move a press. Below left: DFW Movers offers electrostatic painting, in which both the machine to be painted and the paint are charged in such a way that they are strongly attracted to another like a magnet to steel. This is one of the fastest, cleanest, and most cost-efficient ways to brighten and restore used equipment, making it look new.

MANUFACTURING

PROFILES OF COMPANIES AND ORGANIZATIONS

State-of-the-art helicopters from this leading producer of commercial and military vertical lift aircraft fly in more than 120 countries worldwide. Bell Helicopter—a Textron company—sets the industry standard in helicopter rotorcraft design and production as well as in service and support.

Above: Bell Helicopter—a Textron company—is an industry-leading producer of commercial and military, manned and unmanned vertical lift aircraft and the pioneer of the revolutionary tilt-rotor aircraft. Bell's V-22 Osprey, an advanced technology rotorcraft, is used extensively by U.S. military forces. The V-22's phenomenal capabilities—revolutionary speed and range, the ability to carry large payloads over long distances, and self-deployability—make the V-22 an ideal and cost-effective choice for military missions worldwide.

At the forefront of flight technology for more than 50 years, Bell Helicopter is on "the leading edge of vertical lift." More than half of the world's commercial and military helicopters carry the Bell name, giving evidence of this company's credentials as an industry leader. Overall, Bell Helicopter—a Textron company—has delivered more than 37,000 helicopters to customers in 120 countries worldwide.

Bell Takes Flight

Bell Helicopter originally was founded as Bell Aircraft Corporation in 1935. From the beginning, the company set new standards for the industry. In 1946, a Bell helicopter was the first in the world to be certified for commercial use. Then, in 1951, Bell Aircraft created its helicopter division and moved to Fort Worth, Texas. When Textron bought Bell Aircraft in 1960, it renamed the helicopter operation Bell Helicopter Company. Within a few years, Bell Helicopter Company grew into one of Textron's largest divisions.

Among Bell Helicopter's greatest achievements is that it pioneered the tilt-rotor technology. This technology combines the high-speed, long-range qualities of a fixed-wing aircraft with the vertical take-off and hover capabilities of a helicopter. Bell received its first research contract for the tilt-rotor in 1951, and began building this revolutionary aircraft in 1953. This unique aircraft, which flew at twice the speed of an airplane, with three times the payload and five times the range of traditional helicopters, revolutionized aerospace and aircraft. Bell's tilt-rotor technology continues to innovate the industry today.

Flying Smart

Bell Helicopter knows that there is more to owning a helicopter than the mere purchase. The company not only prides itself as the world leader in rotorcraft design and production, it also sets the standard for service and support. With five support centers located strategically around the world, more than 150 Bell Helicopter–approved customer service facilities worldwide for maintenance, and a product support engineering team for each helicopter model on-call 12 hours a day, seven days a week, Bell Helicopter has one of the largest customer support networks in the industry.

The Bell Helicopter Training Academy, also located in Fort Worth, has provided world-class training—certified by the Federal Aviation Administration (FAA)—for more than 50 years. To date, this company has trained more than 100,000 students from every market segment in more than 120 countries. Bell Helicopter's commitment to training follows its same high standards for quality, reliability, and safety to ensure that customers receive the best in products, service, and support—for today and well into the future.

Built on determination, flexibility, and people skills, this Fort Worth–based, woman-owned metal distribution company has established a niche for itself by supplying specialty and hard-to-find metal materials to clients such as race car fabricators and motorcycle manufacturers.

Exemplary customer service, same-day delivery, just-in-time management, and efficient stocking programs define success in many industries. So it is not surprising that these attributes distinguish American Metal Services from its competitors. The success of this Fort Worth–based metal distributor, however, also reflects a combination of fortitude, tenacity, and luck on the part of its founder and owner, Marcha Graham.

Keys to Success: Education, Ingenuity, and Customer Relations

Despite a 13-year career in banking operations, Graham ventured into metal sales at the encouragement of a friend. "From the outset, I really loved it. I was a fast learner and enjoyed talking to people," she says. "When I started, I didn't have a customer base, but I knew how to do research. I could locate hard-to-find materials when others couldn't."

After six years in the metal industry, Graham founded American Metal Services the week of September 11, 2001. Since then, she has developed a niche by supplying hard-to-find metal materials for specialty markets that include race car fabricators and a local motorcycle manufacturer, American IronHorse Motorcycle Company. To generate a cash flow, Graham worked on a "COD" basis.

Graham initially worked out of her home, but when some distributors required her to have a warehouse, she leased space from a customer.

"Our success is based on our rapport with our customers and suppliers," Graham explains. "The cliché, 'It's not what you know but who you know' has some truth. What you know will keep you on top, but who you know can help you get there."

Meeting Challenges: Geared for a Shining Future

The future for American Metal Services looks as bright as a highly polished piece of metal. Today, with one part-time and two full-time employees, American Metal Services supplies some 400,000 pounds of aluminum extrusions annually. The company has also expanded into industrial supplies products such as gloves, saw blades, fittings, coolants, and batteries.

Confident about the future, Graham notes, "Once we proved ourselves as knowledgeable, competitive, and ethical, our customer base grew by word of mouth. Steel distribution is a challenging industry, but I am looking forward to continuing to serve north Texas for years to come."

Above: Entrepreneur Marsha Graham is the founder of American Metal Services.

Specialty Materials and Products

Offering specialty or hard-to-find metal products to a niche market that includes race-car fabricators and a local chopper manufacturer, American Metal Services distributes the following types of metals and supplies:

- Alloy Steel
- Aluminum
- Brass
- Bronze
- Carbon Steel
- Cast Iron
- Copper
- Industrial Supplies
- Nickel
- Plastics
- Stainless Steel
- Tool Steel

Since 1913 this family-owned business—renowned for its responsive, reliable service in collecting, processing, and selling millions of pounds of scrap materials each year—has grown to be one of the largest and most respected recycling companies in the Fort Worth region.

Above left: Gamtex Industries is led by, from left, Iric Gachman, COO; Leon Gachman, CEO emeritus; and Arnold Gachman, CEO, who have steered their family-owned company into the 21st century. Above center: For recycling purposes, Gamtex purchases a wide range of scrap metals, including aluminum, brass, copper, steel, and stainless steel. Above right: Gamtex Industries' transportation fleet has the capacity to move a job of any size, small to large.

Recycling is vital to the safe and economical disposal of solid waste, the conservation of precious natural resources, and the economic production of raw materials. While for many people and companies, recycling is a relatively new concept and practice, Gamtex Industries has been a successful recycling company since 1913.

This Fort Worth–based recycler was founded in Texas by Jacob Gachman, a Russian immigrant. Today, Gamtex Industries—still owned by the family—is one of the largest and most respected recyclers in the region. It operates under the names of Gachman Metals and Recycling, Atlas Iron and Metal, and Jacobs Iron and Metal.

Gamtex Industries collects, processes, and sells millions of pounds of scrap materials each year. Through four generations, the company continually has integrated state-of-the-art technology and automation into its operations, consistently setting high standards for environmental and safety issues.

Recycling to Meet All Business Needs

Processing thousands of tons of metals each month, Gamtex Industries accesses all types of industrial and commercial nonferrous and ferrous scrap metals from the public and private sectors as well as from individuals. These include various materials ranging from titanium metals and alloys to copper and iron. The company then sells the scrap metal to regional, national, and international smelters, specialty markets, and foundries.

Because of its large operation, Gamtex Industries has the ability to tailor recycling solutions to meet the needs of businesses regardless of their size or location. The company has thousands of recycling containers available in all sizes, as well as custom-designed roll-offs and hoppers. Its fleet has the capacity to transport nearly any job, large or small.

Overall, Gamtex Industries has built its reputation on providing quality customer service with efficient and expert recycling solutions to meet its clients' needs.

Iric Gachman, COO of the company, states, "Gamtex prides itself on achieving outstanding regulatory and risk-management compliance. Our people are industry experts, active in the recycling industry both locally and nationally. This adds up to a high quality of service and efficiency that we are able to pass on to our clients."

Manufacturing Company

Precision manufacturing and metallurgical expertise have made this Crowley, Texas–based manufacturer of oil well pumps, parts, and accessories a technological—and industry—leader. Its products, known as the 'Best Pumps in the Oil Patch'®, are used in every oil-producing region of the world.

Harbison-Fischer™ Manufacturing Company, the world's largest manufacturer of subsurface oil well pumps, is the legacy of two men: a mechanical genius and a born salesman. Dixon T. Harbison, superintendent at an oil field machine shop in Illinois, came to Fort Worth in 1928 to find work in the oil industry. And Charles A. Fischer, a young steel company executive, came to Fort Worth from Pittsburgh, Pennsylvania, in 1923 with plans to turn his industry knowledge and sales experience into a successful steel sales agency of his own.

Brought together by a routine sales call, Harbison and Fischer, who admired each other's talents, combined their skills and knowledge as partners in a new company. In 1933 their company began to manufacture and sell oil well pumping equipment. Harbison's gift for precision manufacturing and Fischer's salesmanship convinced customers of the superior quality and economic benefit that their equipment offered. Soon the company moved into larger quarters and began patenting its innovations.

What began as a purely local Fort Worth business was carefully developed and nurtured over the years to become a prominent international company. Harbison-Fischer's mergers, acquisitions, and joint ventures contributed to its growth and product diversity. Among these were the 1985 acquisition of Challenger Process Systems; the 1985 Canadian joint venture (Harbison-Fischer Canada Ltd.), which became a wholly owned subsidiary in 1995; the 1999 acquisition of John N. Martin Manufacturer; the acquisition of Harbison-Fischer's long-time California distributor (Production Services) in 2003, which expanded the company's abilities to support this highly concentrated market; and the 2006 formation of Harbison-Fischer Australia, Pty. Ltd. of Perth.

Since 1982 Harbison-Fischer has occupied a 330,000-square-foot plant in the southern Fort Worth suburb of Crowley. There, a fully equipped metallurgical lab evaluates products; a research and development department studies the most advanced rod pump technology; and an engineering department provides sales support and training. More than 100 field personnel are available to assist distributors and customers with their production problems. In addition, Harbison-Fischer is an American Petroleum Industry Q1- and ISO-certified company, which further attests to Harbison-Fischer's commitment to quality.

Although privately held by the Fischer family since 1972, the company continues to be guided by the founders' vision. Charles K. Fischer Sr., son of founder Charles A. Fischer, is chairman of the board and CEO, while third-generation David Fischer (president and COO) and Charles K. "Kenny" Fischer Jr. (senior vice president) carry the Fischer family tradition of leadership into the 21st century. The company's more than 400 dedicated employees, whose average tenure is 15 years, also carry the founders' torch and keep Harbison-Fischer at the forefront of the industry.

Above: Harbison-Fischer™ Manufacturing Company, which serves the subsurface oil field rod pump market, was cofounded by Dixon T. Harbison (left) and Charles A. Fischer (right).

PROFESSIONAL SERVICES

PROFILES OF COMPANIES AND ORGANIZATIONS

Backed by the strength of more than 300 top attorneys, Jackson Walker LLP is one of the 10 largest Texas-based law firms. The firm's attorneys, who have been retained by Fortune 500 companies, multinational corporations, and other institutions, offer expertise in virtually every area of law.

Above: Jackson Walker LLP's Fort Worth partners, shown here in front of Trinity River, are: (back row, left to right) Gary Ingram, William Jenkins, Keith Branyon, Jay Rutherford, Susan Halsey, and Albon Head; (front row, left to right) James Bradbury, Nikki Fanous, and Sheldon Anisman.

Founded in 1887, Jackson Walker LLP is one of the largest Texas-based law firms. The firm is characterized by its deep Texas roots and a distinguished legal tradition.

With more than 300 attorneys, Jackson Walker regularly represents clients in such areas as energy, international law, corporate and securities, litigation, intellectual property, health care, labor and employment, legislative and regulatory matters, real estate, tax and estate planning, technology, bankruptcy, and aviation law. The firm is dedicated to offering clients superior legal service on a cost-effective basis.

Jackson Walker's Fort Worth office opened in 1988 and is now one of Tarrant County's largest law firms. The office's central location downtown provides convenience for clients and proximity to state and federal courthouses. The Fort Worth office handles matters involving business transactions, health care, land use, environmental, labor and employment, litigation, energy, railroad and transportation, banking, and real estate law.

Many of Jackson Walker's Fort Worth attorneys have been honored as being top attorneys in their practice areas and are known throughout the state and the region for their in-depth experience and knowledge.

Jackson Walker has served the public for more than a century. It supports local communities through civic, charitable, and trade organizations, including the Greater Fort Worth Real Estate Council, the Fort Worth Chamber of Commerce, Downtown Fort Worth Inc., the World Affairs Council of Dallas/Fort Worth, the Greater Fort Worth Commercial Real Estate Women, the Fort Worth Symphony Orchestra, the Fort Worth Opera, Junior Achievement, and the Fort Worth Stock Show Syndicate.

Jackson Walker is proud to be a part of Fort Worth's heritage.

One of the oldest engineering firms in Texas, this company was first recognized for its pioneering efforts in water resources. Today it provides innovative solutions in a broad range of architectural, engineering, and environmental science services to diverse clients throughout the United States.

The professionals at Freese and Nichols, Inc. use the company's vast experience—112 years of accomplishments—as a springboard for fresh approaches to client projects. The group's reputation is that of a "smart idea" firm dedicated to understanding, meeting, and exceeding client expectations with innovative approaches and practical results. With more than 300 employees and offices in Austin, Dallas, Fort Worth, Houston, and San Antonio, the company consistently ranks among the top 500 engineering firms nationwide in *Engineering News-Record.*

Founded in 1894, the scope of Freese and Nichols' expertise has grown as client needs have evolved and technology has advanced. The company initially focused on water supply and sanitary engineering.

Today Freese and Nichols serves municipalities, water districts, river authorities, federal agencies, the military, transportation agencies, educational organizations, and private industry; the company provides:

- Engineering services in the areas of water resources, storm water management, dam design and rehabilitation, pipeline and pump station design, structural engineering, transportation planning and design, and water/wastewater planning, design, treatment, and distribution.
- Program management and construction services, including all services related to planning, design, bid, construction, and post construction.
- Architectural and planning services, including master planning, space planning, and full facility design.
- Environmental science services, with an emphasis on effective strategies for addressing environmental challenges.

The professionals at Freese and Nichols embrace their heritage of excellence as they pursue greater challenges, knowing that their best work and greatest service to their clients still lie ahead.

Above: Freese and Nichols, Inc. provided program management, design, and construction management services for the Skylink automated people mover project at Dallas/Fort Worth International Airport, which debuted in 2005. Below: Freese and Nichols' emergency repair of Morris Sheppard Dam at Possum Kingdom Lake on the Brazos River in Palo Pinto County, Texas, was recognized by the National Society of Professional Engineers as an outstanding engineering achievement in 1990. Freese and Nichols has designed or rehabilitated more than 150 dams in the state of Texas.

Freese and Nichols

Decker, Jones, McMackin, McClane, Hall & Bates, PC

Since 1896, whenever an industry emerged in Texas—oil and gas, real estate, insurance, and technology, for instance—this Fort Worth law firm was there to help clients pioneer the new legal landscape. Today the firm assembles talented attorneys and counselors recognized for their expertise in a wide array of legal specialties.

Above left: Decker Jones traces its origins to 1896, when George Q. McGown (far left) entered the practice of law in Fort Worth. He soon met success representing a variety of local and national businesses. He was later joined in the practice by his sons H. T. McGown (center), and George Q. McGown Jr. (right). Above right: Today the firm's shareholders include, from left, (first row) Janet Hahn, Jim Stripling, Randy Hall, Chuck Milliken, and Jeff Storie; (second row) Geoff Mantooth, Brad Rice, Rob Kelly, and Brian Yost; and (third row) Mark Dugan, Dan Bates, and Gary Moates.

At Decker Jones, innovation is an old-fashioned idea. From the firm's beginning more than a century ago, the practice has remained focused on helping clients find new ways to succeed. When the discovery of oil in nearby Ranger gave birth to the west Texas oil boom in 1917, the firm's oil and gas practice guided many of the early wildcatters into largely uncharted legal territory. Today Decker Jones's board-certified oil and gas counsel represents many of the Fort Worth Basin's most successful exploration operations as these enterprises respond to opportunities offered by the area's newfound natural gas reserves.

In the 1950s, before the development of condominium law, the firm's real estate lawyers pioneered legal structures for the sale of high-rise apartment units . Attorneys in the firm's real estate, banking, and construction group continue to be recognized among the best and brightest in the expanding north Texas market. The firm's business and corporate section helped many local entrepreneurs break new ground and extend their reach into national and international markets throughout the 1960s and 1970s. This tradition continues as Decker Jones business, employment, and tax counsel provide leadership to businesses and individuals in structuring ventures, negotiating and documenting transactions, and dealing with the everyday issues of compliance in a fast-paced global business environment.

Decker Jones was the first Fort Worth–based business law firm to offer a full range of intellectual property law services. The firm's intellectual property (IP) practice group provides comprehensive trademark coverage to clients through its worldwide network of trademark professionals. The group's patent counsel has secured protection for hundreds of inventions, covering a wide variety of fields. Decker Jones IP transaction lawyers routinely represent companies and individuals with copyright, trademark, or patent concerns in the negotiation of agreements—which range from trademark and patent licenses to recording and publishing contracts. The Decker Jones brand protection unit is a leader in the fight against the counterfeiting of branded products, and it polices the Texas markets on behalf of many of the world's leading brands.

Dispute resolution has always been a cornerstone of the Decker Jones service model. The firm's litigation practice group is widely recognized for its effective representation of hospitals and health care professionals, especially in the defense of medical malpractice claims, and for the defense of product liability and toxic tort claims. The Decker Jones staff of board-certified civil trial lawyers has hundreds of jury trials to its credit, and its members' collective experience includes a wide variety of commercial, construction, employment, and IP law litigation.

For the lawyers of Decker Jones, innovation is as old-fashioned as the firm's other core values: integrity, hard work, and personal service.

REAL ESTATE, CONSTRUCTION, DEVELOPMENT, AND PLANNING SERVICES

PROFILES OF COMPANIES AND ORGANIZATIONS

Crescent Real Estate Equities Company

Headquartered in Fort Worth, this real estate investment trust owns and manages a portfolio of premier office properties in select markets in Dallas, Houston, Austin, Denver, Miami, and Las Vegas and also invests in resort residential developments, in destination resorts, and in Canyon Ranch®.

Above: Crescent Real Estate Equities Company co-owns three prominent office towers in Dallas: The Crescent® (foreground), the financial center of the Southwest; Trammell Crow Center (left background), situated in the heart of the downtown arts district; and Fountain Place® (right background), a dramatically sculpted tower rising from a tree-lined oasis of fountains, pools, and flowers.

Crescent Real Estate Equities Company is a $6 billion real estate investment trust based in Fort Worth. Led by cofounder, vice chairman and chief executive officer John C. Goff, Crescent owns and manages a portfolio of premier office buildings in select markets across the country in cities such as Dallas, Houston, Austin, Denver, Miami, and Las Vegas. Crescent also holds significant investments in destination resorts such as the Fairmont Sonoma Mission Inn & Spa®, in Sonoma, California; in resort residential developments in unique locations such as Lake Tahoe, California; Vail Valley, Colorado; and Scottsdale, Arizona; and in the wellness lifestyle leader, Canyon Ranch®. In addition, Crescent is actively developing several projects across the United States, including The Ritz-Carlton, Dallas® and The Residences at The Ritz-Carlton, Dallas®.

Trading on the New York Stock Exchange since 1994 under the symbol CEI, Crescent achieves attractive returns on invested capital by capitalizing on its award-winning office-management platform through investments in demand-driven markets where job growth expectations surpass the national average. In all, Crescent owns and manages, through subsidiaries and joint ventures, a portfolio of 73 premier office buildings totaling 30 million square feet. Some of Crescent's most familiar assets include Fountain Place® and The Crescent® in Dallas, Greenway Plaza in Houston, and Hughes Center, just off the Strip in Las Vegas.

Crescent offers state-of-the-art office workplace environments which are designed for efficiency and cost-effective operations. The size of Crescent's portfolio, particularly in cities such as Dallas, Houston, and Las Vegas, where it is the largest owner of Class A office space, enables Crescent to maximize cost efficiencies for its office customers.

"Our customers are our most important asset, and we strive to go above and beyond their expectations," says Denny Alberts, president and chief operating officer. "They want world-class office space at a fair price. They want award-winning customer service. They want innovative technology and amenities. We give them what they want and more with The Crescent Distinction."

The Crescent Distinction is the cornerstone of Crescent's success, making it possible for the company to form joint ventures for almost half of its office portfolio with institutional partners that value Crescent's exceptional office-operating platform. Individually, these joint ventures increase equity returns by 300 to 600 basis points. Collectively, they provide the long-term growth that shareholders and institutional partners want.

Crescent's office customers agree that the company is committed to excellent customer service. In 2006, for the fifth consecutive year, Crescent was awarded the National Commercial Real Estate Customer Service Award for Excellence for the service it provides by CEL & Associates, one of the largest surveyors of customer satisfaction in the real estate industry. The award reflects Crescent's ongoing commitment to customer service as evidenced by its office customers' vote of confidence.

Crescent's commitment to its customers extends to its investments in lifestyle-related businesses such as resort residential developments in spectacular locations of natural beauty

and recreational opportunities. Crescent forms partnerships with superior management teams in each endeavor to focus primarily on the buying power and preferences of aging baby boomers as they seek both a refuge from and a reward for their demanding careers and as they pursue healthy, active lifestyles. Crescent's lifestyle business includes investments in the award-winning Desert Mountain community in Scottsdale, Arizona, and in luxury communities in the Vail Valley of Colorado and in the north Lake Tahoe area of California. The company's lifestyle business also includes its 48 percent interest in Canyon Ranch, a company that champions healthful lifestyles and is expanding its brand to include communities where residents can make healthy lifestyle choices in everyday living. Canyon Ranch Living® communities, such as the one under construction in Miami Beach, Florida, feature beautifully appointed luxury condominiums; superb spa and fitness facilities; integrative wellness services with physicians, nutritionists, and other practitioners; a restaurant that serves healthy Canyon Ranch cuisine; and a hotel.

Another aspect of Crescent's lifestyle business is its development of The Ritz-Carlton, Dallas and The Residences at The Ritz-Carlton, Dallas, adjacent to Crescent's namesake office towers in uptown Dallas. Revitalization in Dallas's downtown and uptown markets has resulted in a demand for high-end living accommodations, and the hotel and residences will offer luxury unlike anything Dallas has ever seen. Residences range from one-bedroom homes to penthouses, and all offer views of the city skyline. Homeowners will be well served by The Ritz-Carlton, Dallas staff and have access to all the personal services of the hotel. Slated to open in September 2007, the 217-room hotel features a gourmet restaurant and bar with world renowned chef Dean Fearing, as well as meeting space, a state-of-the-art spa, and one of the largest ballrooms in the city.

Crescent is also committed to serving its communities. The company's 725 employees, 200 of whom are based at Crescent's Fort Worth office, have the opportunity to volunteer and participate in Crescent's signature community program, FACES of Change®. This unique adopt-a-school program is the heart of Crescent's community outreach. Through the program, Crescent supports its communities by way of philanthropic partnerships with elementary schools in the area. Since FACES began in 1997, Crescent has worked in partnership with 68 elementary schools, raised more than $2 million, and volunteered more than 45,000 hours. In 2006, a major initiative with Crescent's partner school in Fort Worth raised $50,000 to build a playground and improve the playground area.

In the spirit of the company's commitment to children and education, and to celebrate the milestone of its 10th anniversary, Crescent donated $10,000 to a library in each of its major markets across the country. In Fort Worth, this initial commitment led to a more extensive project—the adoption of the Northside Branch Library. "As we learned how much local families used this library, I personally became inspired by what we might be able to accomplish," says Goff. "This was a well-used, well-loved, and well worn library, and if we could improve the facilities to better serve the library patrons, the impact would be lasting." For the project, Crescent leveraged its relationships with its contractors, vendors, and customers to provide renovations worth more than $80,000. The library was painted inside and out, new carpeting and improved lighting were installed, and a colorful redesigned children's area was created and now greets every patron. Crescent makes a point to go beyond its common business goals in order to help improve its communities and make a difference in the lives of children.

Both Crescent and Fort Worth have experienced tremendous growth since Crescent's inception in 1994. "Fort Worth has seen remarkable economic growth over the past several years, and the best is yet to come," Goff says. "Crescent operates in many great cities across the country, yet Fort Worth has an appeal all its own. Crescent is proud to call this dynamic and vibrant city 'home.'"

Above left: Crescent owns Mira Vista Golf Club in southwest Fort Worth. The club's championship golf course winds through the natural beauty of this 625-acre private community, complementing the development's luxury homes. Above center: Since 1994, 777 Main Street in Fort Worth has been the home of Crescent's headquarters. This 955,000-square-foot, Class A office property, known as Carter Burgess Plaza, is just one of the many premier office properties in Crescent's portfolio. Above right: John C. Goff, CEO of Crescent Real Estate Equities Company, reads to children from Versia Williams Elementary School in Fort Worth. Crescent and the school work in partnership through FACES of Change®, the company's signature adopt-a-school program.

SEDALCO Construction Services

By building relationships with its clients—in addition to the impressive buildings it constructs for them—this full-service contracting and construction company earns much of its revenues through repeat business, and garners awards from organizations as diverse as the American Institute of Architects to the U.S. Navy.

Above: SEDALCO Construction Services projects include (left) One Colinas Crossing in Farmers Branch, Texas, where i2 Technologies, Inc. is headquartered, and (right) the University of North Texas Health Science Center in Fort Worth, Texas.

SEDALCO Construction Services is a full-service regional general contracting and construction management firm formed in Fort Worth in 1983. Annual revenues have placed SEDALCO as one of the top firms serving the Texas market and the contiguous 48 states. With approximately 70 percent of annual revenues being achieved by contract sales from past clients, SEDALCO's emphasis on "building relationships with our clients, not just their buildings" has been a significant ongoing key to its success. As a testament to this, SEDALCO has been regularly recognized locally, regionally, and nationally for award-winning buildings, processes, and people.

While historically SEDALCO has always recruited the leading quality professionals in the industry, the firm places a major emphasis on the recruitment and development of new professionals coming out of university programs throughout the region. To facilitate this effort, SEDALCO maintains leadership on the construction science advisory boards of Texas A&M University, Texas Tech University, and the University of Oklahoma. Additionally, SEDALCO has been a key member of the Construction Education Foundation (CEF) since its inception.

While SEDALCO recognizes the absolute importance of its team being formed from the very best people, it also believes that good people need the best support. So every major component of the construction process has a developed proven method of monitored checks and balances to ensure the total success of the project. SEDALCO prides itself on leaving nothing to chance or experience alone. Verifiable and demonstrable methods of cost analysis, budgeting, and estimating, as well as scheduling, safety, and quality control, are all managed systemic processes—or, as SEDALCO puts it, "The best people with the best tools."

As proof of its approach, SEDALCO has received the following awards and accolades:

- Multiple Project Awards of Construction Excellence—*Texas Construction* magazine, AIA, AGC, ABC, ASA
- Project Team of the Year—ASA
- Project of the Year—ASA
- National Safety Excellence—AGC, ABC, Business Roundtable
- Contractor of the Year—U.S. Navy ROICC, Barksdale AFB
- Employer of the Year—Fort Worth Rotary Club
- Top 100 Private Companies—*Fort Worth Business Press*
- Small Business of the Year—Fort Worth Chamber of Commerce
- Accredited Quality Contractor—ABC
- Quality in Construction—AIA, Fort Worth chapter

The future of SEDALCO is unlimited. The company will continue as a recognized leader in the construction industry, maintaining an environment that encourages constant improvement in the quality of its services as well as in its ability to identify and meet or exceed its customers' requirements and expectations. SEDALCO Construction Services believes that satisfied clients provide the best advertisement: "Proven performance over perception . . . Talk to our customers!"

NAI Huff Partners

One of the largest commercial real estate firms in the Fort Worth–Dallas marketplace, this company is the leader in the finalization of Tarrant County commercial brokerage transactions. The virtues of leadership—integrity, loyalty, intelligence—are integral to NAI Huff Partners' longstanding relationships and powerful track record of results.

Above: With a staff of seasoned veterans in every area of commercial real estate services, NAI Huff Partners offers clients creative, specialized services for all real estate needs, from buying, selling, and leasing to developing and property management. For additional information, contact NAI Huff Partners at 300 Commerce Street, Fort Worth, Texas 76102; phone: 817-877-4433; fax: 817-870-2826; or visit the NAI Huff Partners Web site at www.huffpartners.com.

Fort Worth-based NAI Huff Partners covers all aspects of commercial real estate: office, industrial, investment, retail, hospitality, land, and property management. With 23 brokers including 9 principals, the partners alone bring over 150 years of combined experience to the company. NAI Huff Partners is the largest commercial real estate firm in Tarrant County, completing more than 60 percent of the commercial real estate transactions there in 2005.

Established in 1986, the firm was originally called Huff, Brous, McDowell, and Montesi. In 2000 the firm merged with Stoneleigh, a Dallas firm, and affiliated with NAI Global, a managed network of independent commercial real estate brokerage firms with over 300 offices in the United States and 40 other countries.

In 2005 a new entity, Huff Partners LP, was formed, retaining the NAI affiliation with exclusive rights to represent the western half of the Greater Fort Worth–Dallas area; the counties of Tarrant, Parker, Johnson, and Hood, plus a portion of Denton County; and the cities of Fort Worth, Arlington, the Mid-Cities, Grapevine, Colleyville, Southlake, and Denton.

NAI Huff Partners has an open, family-oriented atmosphere that promotes broker interaction and offers vast experience in all aspects of commercial real estate, from buying, selling, and leasing to tenant representation, new development, joint ventures, property management, and construction services. Available sales and lease aids include CoStar, MapInfo, Realtrac, LoopNet, ProCalc, ACT and Air Photo USA.

Company president M. G. "Bud" Smith says, "Real estate is very important to our clients' success. We invest the time and bring the expertise, interest, and ability to ask the right questions, find the best answers, and then manage the details of our clients' needs."

NAI Huff Partners also maintains a strong community presence. The firm generously supports many public endeavors through the donation of professional time and expertise and provides monetary support and participates in numerous charitable organizations.

Projected growth in Tarrant and surrounding counties is certain to provide excellent investment opportunities. NAI Huff Partners will remain at the forefront of this growth by continually adding proven brokers; and by hiring top young associates, providing them with professional training, and having them become part of a broker team. This ensures that the company has the people and processes to meet its clients' future real estate needs.

Jack Huff, the name partner and one of the original firm's founders, sums up the company's success: "Having the right partner at the end of the day, a partner you can trust, is all about confidence, integrity, and relationships that will last for years to come. We build long-term relationships through superior performance, keeping our clients' interests first, and working harder than the competition."

a marvel of urban revitalization—offers something for practically everyone: wonderful restaurants and entertainment options, unique shops and boutiques, a premier business address, and upscale residences.

Above: Unique and eclectic shops are sprinkled throughout the Sundance Square district, including Earth Bones, Jos. A. Bank, MoonStruck, Parfumerie Marie Antoinette and Spa and Leddy's Ranch in Sundance, pictured here. Right: Sundance Square offers a myriad of dining choices, including everything from fire-grilled cheeseburgers to the finest in cowboy cuisine. Taverna Pizzeria and Risotteria, pictured here, offers both authentic Italian fare and cutting-edge Italian cuisine.

Widely acknowledged as one of the most exciting downtown areas in Texas, Sundance Square is a 20-block shopping and entertainment district that gives new meaning to the term "multi-use." For countless visitors and locals, Sundance Square is the best place in the city for dining and entertainment. For businesses of all sizes and types, Sundance Square is an address that provides all the elements for success. The district is also home to many residents who love the convenience and vitality of downtown living.

Named for Butch Cassidy's partner, the Sundance Kid, this downtown development has prospered through visionary urban planning. Major efforts were made to preserve the historical integrity of downtown Fort Worth, from the vintage bricks on Main Street to the careful restoration of structures built in the early 20th century. Thanks to generous sidewalks and street-facing storefronts, the area is also very friendly for pedestrians. A stroll through Sundance Square today—day or night—reveals a bustling street scene that includes people of all ages and walks of life.

Tempting and Awe Inspiring

Sundance Square is home to dozens of excellent restaurants—from cowboy cuisine at Reata Restaurant to Asian delicacies at P.F. Chang's China Bistro, from Mexican food at Mi Cocina to fresh sushi at Piranha's Killer Sushi.

Moving from fine dining to the fine arts, the Nancy Lee and Perry R. Bass Performance Hall is one of the finest places in America to see a show. Its architecture is spectacular, highlighted by a pair of 48-foot limestone angels on the building's facade. Equally awe inspiring are the acoustics inside this 2,056-seat performance art landmark.

Other entertainment options abound, including live music at multiple nightspots, the latest movies presented on 20 screens at two AMC Theatres, live theater at the Jubilee Theatre and the Circle Theatre, and acclaimed improvisational comedy by the Four Day Weekend troupe.

Shopping is another favorite activity in Sundance Square, where unique specialty boutiques line the busy sidewalks.

Award Winning

In 1985, Sundance Square received the prestigious James C. Howland Award from the National League of Cities. In 2005, the Fort Worth Chamber of Commerce bestowed its Spirit of Enterprise Award on Sundance Square in recognition of its many contributions.

As Fort Worth continues to grow, Sundance Square will continue to play an important part in the city's future. For additional information, visit Sundance Square's Web site at www.sundancesquare.com.

Mercantile Center

By offering access to local, national, and international markets as well as access to substantial tax incentives, this premier Fort Worth business park has become a strategic location for companies looking to expand their reach and increase their revenues.

Some 40 years ago, most people didn't give a second thought to a patch of dormant farmland in north central Tarrant County, Texas. A visionary group of people with a passion for development, however, recognized its potential to be something more. They believed that one day this land would be an ideal location to attract businesses to the Fort Worth area. That vision evolved into Mercantile Center, a 1,500-acre master-planned business park for industrial, office, and service facilities.

Located on Interstate 35 West, one-half mile south of Interstate 820 North, and just minutes from Dallas/Fort Worth International Airport (DFW) and downtown Fort Worth, Mercantile Center is indeed strategically positioned.

It is also situated in an Enterprise Zone, a Foreign Trade Zone, and a Triple Freeport Exemption area. These tax incentives can amount to a significant savings for the center's tenants.

As a result, Mercantile Center has attracted some of the country's most successful companies and organizations, including Citigroup, Sara Lee Food & Beverage, Origen Financial, Cash America International, Dillard's, Sprint, Countrywide Home Loans, and the Federal Aviation Administration.

The business park's success has been bolstered by Fort Worth's tremendous growth in the past 25 years as well.

"Fort Worth offers effective city planning, excellent demographics from which businesses can recruit employees, and a very favorable business climate," says Brian Randolph, Mercantile vice president.

"Mercantile Center has enjoyed a steady growth over the past decade," he says. "We are fully committed to the City of Fort Worth and the surrounding areas, and plan to continue to develop the center into a top quality business park. We believe the future of Fort Worth is a bright one, and Mercantile Center is poised to play a prominent role in our community's future growth."

Above left: Saxon Mortgage, provider of home loans and refinancing services, is just one of the many successful companies that has chosen Mercantile Center as its home base. Above right: Spanning more than 1,500 acres, Mercantile Center offers prime industrial and office locations within minutes of downtown Fort Worth.

Dunaway Associates, L.P.

This leading civil engineering firm, which has developed numerous well-known projects in the Fort Worth area, is dedicated to providing clients with the best possible expertise and service, full resources, and excellent professional relationships, in accordance with its slogan: 'Listen. Envision. Execute.'

Left: Dunaway Associates, L.P. is owned and managed by, from left, Toby K. Ford, P.E., vice president; Thomas O.Huffhines, P.E., president; and Thomas S. Galbreath, A.S.L.A., executive vice president. Right: Among the accomplishments of the company is the headquarters building of Pier 1 Imports, in downtown Fort Worth.

Founded in 1956 by James R. Dunaway Sr., Dunaway Associates, L.P. is one of the Southwest's leading engineering firms, offering a full range of civil engineering services including land-use analysis and master planning, zoning, land and site development, surveying, drainage and water resource management, water and sewer utilities, street and roadway engineering, environmental services, and landscape architecture.

The firm was acquired in 2003 by Thomas O. Huffhines, P.E., now the company's president; Thomas S. Galbreath, A.S.L.A., executive vice president; and Toby K. Ford, P.E., vice president, who together manage a multifaceted team of experienced and licensed professionals. The diverse talents of the firm's in-house specialists combined with the targeted expertise of trusted subconsultants have made Dunaway an engineering company of choice for residential, retail, commercial, industrial, educational, cultural, municipal, and transportation projects.

Some of the company's notable accomplishments include Walsh Ranch, a 7,275-acre master-planned community in west Fort Worth; the Grand Marc; Doctors Surgery Center at Huguley Memorial Medical Center; South of Seventh (So7), a mixed-use development located between the Fort Worth Cultural District and the Central Business District; and in downtown Fort Worth, a mixed-use development at Texas Christian University, as well as the Pier 1 Imports headquarters, a 21-story high-rise building.

Dunaway Associates and several of its staff members are registered and licensed in the state of Texas as engineering, environmental sciences, landscaping, planning, and surveying professionals. However, more than the firm's impeccable credentials have led to its success over the past half century. Equally important is the company's commitment to open dialogue throughout all phases of a project—a philosophy of collaboration adhered to throughout Dunaway Associates' many engineering disciplines and with its clientele. Dunaway strives for a successful union of its clients' objectives and for responsible stewardship of the environment, with the ultimate goal of improving the community at large.

As a corporate citizen of Fort Worth, Dunaway Associates is equally committed to supporting the city it calls home. The firm makes charitable contributions of time and resources, striving to enhance the well-being of people in the Fort Worth area through its ongoing support of organizations such as the Komen Race for the Cure, the Cook Children's Medical Center, the Fort Worth YMCA, and the Lena Pope Home.

Midwest Wrecking Co. of Texas, Inc.

With a reputation for quality work, this longtime Fort Worth company tackles the unique requirements of each job with the equipment and personnel to meet critical time schedules, the experience and knowledge to solve tough structural matters, and the ability to complete any demolition project safely and efficiently.

Midwest Wrecking Co. of Texas, Inc. was founded in Fort Worth in March 1984 and incorporated in the state of Texas in April 1986. In August 2003, two longtime employees, David Densmore and Brian Choate, purchased the company from its founder, Ben E. Kates Jr. Today Midwest Wrecking Co. of Texas, Inc. has 35 employees, many of whom have been in the demolition industry for their entire career.

Midwest Wrecking Co. of Texas is engaged full time in the demolition and/or dismantling of commercial, industrial, and residential structures, primarily in Tarrant County and the surrounding counties. The company works on from 150 to 200 projects per year, generating approximately $6 million in annual gross sales. Approximately 60 percent of Midwest Wrecking Co. of Texas projects include total or partial structural demolition of a building, while the balance includes selective demolition of structures that are being remodeled. The company specializes in difficult projects requiring the kind of intense planning and coordination that only an experienced team of dedicated professionals can achieve.

Because of its reputation as a leader in its industry, Midwest Wrecking Co. of Texas has been fortunate enough to work on most of the high profile projects that have occurred in downtown Fort Worth. These include:

- demolition of the Ripley Arnold housing complex for the RadioShack corporate campus;
- demolition of the Calvary Cathedral Church for the Pier 1 corporate headquarters;
- interior selective demolition of the former Bank One for The Tower;
- interior and exterior selective demolition of the former Montgomery Ward building for the Montgomery Plaza development;
- interior and exterior selective demolition of the former Baker Building for the Bob R. Simpson Building;
- demolition of the 44-acre Riverside Village Apartment Community for the Sierra Vista housing development;
- interior selective demolition of the former Spaghetti Warehouse in the Fort Worth Stockyards for the XTO Energy office expansion; and
- implosion of the 33-story Landmark Tower, the tallest building ever demolished in the state of Texas.

Paralleling the local economy, the company has enjoyed slow, steady growth over the more than 20 years since it began. Although many opportunities for growth exist statewide as well as nationally, Midwest Wrecking Co. of Texas, Inc. intends to remain focused on the Fort Worth metroplex for its continued success.

Above, all photos: Midwest Wrecking Co. of Texas, Inc. handled the implosion in March 2006 of the 33-story Landmark Tower in downtown Fort Worth—the tallest building ever demolished in the state of Texas.

Ajax Glass and Mirror Company

A well-known member of the Fort Worth business community since 1945, this family-owned glass, mirror, and builders' hardware company has earned a reputation as an industry leader in residential housing by delivering quality products and services for three generations.

Above: Buddy Moses (left) and Arthur Moses (right)—the sons of R. D. Moses, who was one of this company's original principals—continue to guide the Ajax Glass and Mirror Company in the spirit of their father's creed: "Listen to what customers have to say and always treat them fairly."

The family-owned and -operated Ajax Glass and Mirror Company, founded by James Cohen, has served the Fort Worth, Texas, region for more than 60 years and is recognized as one of the area's leading glass firms. With its industry expertise and commitment to customer service, the company serves both homeowners and home builders from its 32,000-square-foot facility and showroom in Fort Worth. Ajax Glass specializes in the professional installation and repair of window glass, commercial storefronts, and custom-designed shower doors and mirrors, as well as framed mirrors, furniture tops, etched glass, builders' hardware, and related products.

From its founding in 1945, Ajax Glass grew and changed along with its city. Located in downtown Fort Worth, the company originally focused on automotive glass installation. Then in the 1950s, the founder's son-in-law, R. D. Moses, joined the company and saw the potential in expanding its services and products to supply the growing residential market. The company began offering homeowners and home builders windows, mirrors, shower doors, and furniture tops, and ultimately the housing market became Ajax Glass's core business.

As sales steadily increased and the business continually grew, a new location was needed. In 1975 Ajax Glass moved to Fort Worth's West Vickery Boulevard, to a new 10,000-square-foot building with a 1,200-square-foot display showroom. By this time the company was serving all of Fort Worth and many surrounding communities. Ajax Glass continued to focus on providing excellent workmanship, competitive pricing, and reliable customer service, which brought further growth, and in 1978 the facility was expanded to more than double its size.

The late 1970s also brought a new generation of the family into the company. R. D. Moses' sons, Arthur and Buddy Moses, joined Ajax Glass, learning the technical side of the business. They have carried on their father's customer relations creed: "Listen to what customers have to say and always treat them fairly."

Sales continued to grow, and in the 1980s the business was again expanded, adding to its services with commercial storefront installation and to its products with builders' hardware.

Today, as a longtime, integral part of the community, Ajax Glass and Mirror Company is often called upon for projects that other firms might not handle. A new, larger facility located in the heart of Forth Worth's southwest and west side is projected for completion in 2007. The company's well-trained staff, comprising 50 employees, travels the entire metroplex in a fleet of 19 service vehicles—still helping to build Fort Worth, offering new products, professional installation, and superior service.

Williams Trew Real Estate Services

A full-service approach to selling and listing real estate, combined with advanced technology and innovative marketing strategies, has given one of Fort Worth's top real estate agencies a reputation for professional service that consistently exceeds customer expectations.

The owners and agents of Williams Trew Real Estate Services share a love of Fort Worth and the people who live there. They are dedicated to serving the needs of the families and individuals they represent, providing the kind of valuable insight and advice that can only come from agents who work in their own hometown.

Founded in 2000 by Joan Trew and Martha Williams, two of Tarrant County's top residential real estate agents, the company began with a team of 15 agents in one office on Camp Bowie Boulevard. Trew and Williams, along with Marshall Boyd, managing partner and COO, have created an agency with 80 sales associates that handle a wide array of real estate requests.

Expanded Services

From the outset, the owners dreamed of developing a full-service agency, so in 2004 they expanded their services to include property management. Today, Williams Trew agents handle property leasing and management for investors throughout Tarrant County. The division, Williams Trew Property Management, also provides full real estate brokerage services, buyer representation, senior market consultation services, and more.

As a member of Leading Real Estate Companies of the World, a network of nearly 700 top independent U.S. real estate firms, Williams Trew also helps clients with relocation services, including buying or selling a home, mortgage banking, and real estate broker referrals.

The company's Farm and Ranch division, added in 2005, is staffed by brokers who understand rural property issues, such as land-tax status, mineral rights, surface water rights, and animal and agricultural restrictions.

The Urban division, also created in 2005, helps residents find a home in downtown Fort Worth, where shops, restaurants, nightlife, museums, and the arts are within walking distance.

A Role in the Community

The professionals at Williams Trew Real Estate Services take pride in serving the residents of the unique city of Fort Worth, with its dynamic real estate market. They play an active role in the community, serving on numerous corporate, civic, and cultural boards, including the Fort Worth Chamber of Commerce. The company also supports charitable organizations, including the Tarrant County Child Protective Services, the American Red Cross, Presbyterian Night Shelter of Tarrant County, and Fort Worth Area Habitat for Humanity.

Above: Leading Williams Trew Real Estate Services are Martha Williams, left, Marshall Boyd, center, and Joan Trew, right. Since 2000, they have turned Williams Trew into one of Fort Worth's premier full-service real estate agencies.

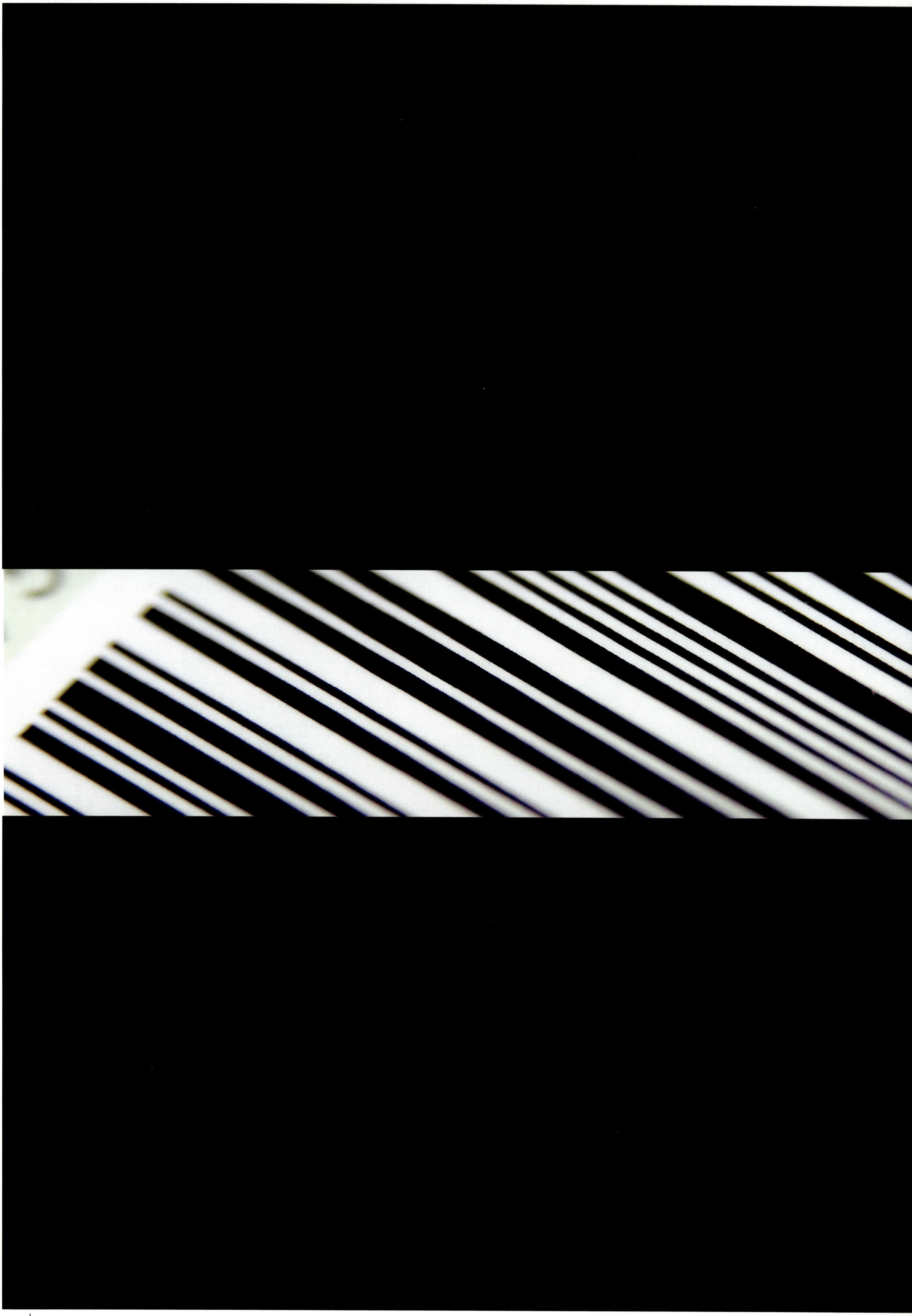

RETAIL, SALES, AND CONSUMER GOODS & SERVICES

PROFILES OF COMPANIES AND ORGANIZATIONS

this socially conscious company—one of North America's largest specialty retailers of home furnishings and accessories from around the world—offers customers something new with every store visit.

Pier 1 Imports is a global company in every sense of the word. It operates stores across the United States—as well as in Puerto Rico, Canada, and Mexico—and features products from more than 50 countries worldwide. Pier 1 also continually strives to improve the lives of thousands of people through its philanthropic partnerships at the international, national, and local levels.

For more than 40 years, Pier 1 has offered excellent value in distinct casual home furnishings and décor; an ever-changing assortment of merchandise to personalize the home; and professional integrity in its treatment of customers, vendors, and associates. For fiscal year 2006, the company saw net sales of nearly $2 billion. In addition, Pier 1 currently has 1,200 stores throughout North America, and employs 17,000 people worldwide. Some 1,000 employees work at the company's headquarters at Pier 1 Place in Fort Worth, Texas.

Pier 1's strategies for success also include the timely introduction of creative marketing campaigns, the employment of knowledgeable and helpful associates who share their enthusiasm with customers, and a continual flow of unique merchandise. The company's merchandise ranges from small decorative accessories such as candles, vases, and picture frames to full-size upholstered furniture, armoires of hand-carved woods, large-scale urns, and eclectic wall décor. Every year, up to 75 percent of Pier 1's product mix is newly introduced, giving shoppers reason to return again and again.

Right: In 2004, Pier 1 Imports moved into its new 460,000-square-foot corporate headquarters, which is located on 12 acres along the Trinity River in Fort Worth, Texas. One of the first key buildings in the city's proposed riverfront redevelopment project, this complex features a conference center, an information systems training center, and amenities for associates such as a fitness center, a walking trail, and an on-site café.

Bringing Home Style

The process that brings special items from all over the world to Pier 1 stores is a long and interesting journey that begins with buyers who help to develop as well as import goods from points near and far. Pier 1 buyers work with designers abroad and with the company's trend development team to create proprietary designs as well as to forecast merchandise trends, develop product patterns and colors, and design packaging that successfully presents the products. Complementing the work of Pier 1 buyers is the company's visual merchandising team, which creates the appealing environment found in

Pier 1 stores. The team's designs make Pier 1 stores easy to navigate for shoppers and create a streamlined, organized look with vignettes so that customers can envision how merchandise will look in their own homes.

Giving Far and Near

In addition to its retail reach, Pier 1 has a broad humanitarian reach. In 2006, Pier 1 was named "Outstanding Corporation" from the Association of Fundraising Professionals for its philanthropic and community outreach programs. Since 1985, more than $30 million has been contributed by Pier 1 to international, national, and local philanthropic organizations, including UNICEF (United Nations Children's Fund; Pier 1 has donated more than $24 million to date); the Susan G. Komen Breast Cancer Foundation (Pier 1 has donated more than $4 million in the last 15 years); and, locally, the United Way of Tarrant County and the E. M. Daggett Elementary School in Fort Worth, Pier 1's Adopt-A-School partner.

For Pier 1's partnership with the E. M. Daggett Elementary School, the company was honored with the Fort Worth Independent School District's Exemplary Partnership Award three times. Pier 1 associates support the school through various works, including the Daggett Elementary Clothing Closet, the Spikes for Tikes charity golf tournament, and educational programs.

The Pier 1 Story

The products displayed at Pier 1 have come a long way—and Pier 1 stores have come a long way as well. The company continually looks for ways to stay fresh and new in order to offer unique home décor items that fit customers' lifestyles.

1962 The first Pier 1 Imports store opens in San Mateo, California; popular items on display include beanbag chairs, love beads, and incense.

1966 Corporate headquarters are established in Fort Worth, Texas, and Pier 1 has 16 stores with a variety of merchandise.

1970 Pier 1 becomes a public company; two years later, Pier 1 (NYSE: PIR) has 124 stores, including stores in Australia and Europe.

1979 A Pier 1 store in Royal Oak, Michigan, is the first to reach $1 million in annual sales.

1985 With 265 stores, the company hones its image as a retailer of quality, unique home furnishings and decorative accessories; a plan is launched to double the number of stores over five years.

1988 The Pier 1 Preferred Card is introduced, and within six years Preferred Card sales reach $100 million.

1993 Pier 1 expands into Puerto Rico, begins a partnership with a chain of import stores in the United Kingdom, and opens boutiques in Mexico.

1999 Chairman and CEO Marvin Girouard creates a pricing and merchandising repositioning strategy that puts Pier 1 back in touch with its core customers and leads to fiscal 1999 sales of more than $1 billion —a net income increase of 43 percent.

2001 The company acquires Cargo Furniture and Home and turns it into Cargokids, specializing in fashionable, value-oriented furniture and clothing for children; in 2004, Cargokids is renamed Pier 1 Kids, with expanded merchandise.

2003 The opening of the Summerlin, Nevada, store marks Pier 1's 1,000th North American store.

2004 The company moves into its corporate headquarters at Pier 1 Place, in Fort Worth's proposed riverfront improvement project. The complex includes conference, training, and fitness facilities.

2006 A new merchandising direction called Pier 1 Modern Craftsman is introduced to help the company regain its niche in the home furnishings industry while it continues to feature specialty home décor items.

Above left: The first Pier 1 store was opened in San Mateo, California, in 1962. Above right: In the early years, exotic goods imported from around the world were delivered to Pier 1 stores in small trucks like this one.

As one of the most trusted consumer electronics specialty retailers, this Fort Worth–based company has more than 6,000 stores and dealer outlets and nearly 800 wireless kiosks throughout the United States, Mexico, and Canada.

Above: RadioShack Corporation, one of the nation's largest electronics retailers, traces its lineage to a Fort Worth leather company that was started in 1919.

It is estimated that 94 percent of all Americans live or work within five minutes of a RadioShack store or dealer outlet.

With more than 6,000 stores and nearly 800 wireless kiosks across the country, RadioShack offers a retail service concept that is unique. It provides simple, cost-effective solutions for people's routine electronics needs and distinct electronics wants.

At RadioShack, regarded as one of the nation's most trusted consumer electronics retailers, sales associates consistently help customers by demystifying technology. Then they help them select the best products to suit their needs—from batteries and audiovisual cables to wireless communications devices, digital imaging and home entertainment components, and LCD television sets.

Built On a Shoestring

The RadioShack story began in Fort Worth in 1919. Two friends, Norton Hinckley and Dave L. Tandy, pooled their resources to open a business, the Hinckley-Tandy Leather Company. They sold leather shoelaces, soles, and heels to cobblers in the Fort Worth area.

Two years later, in Boston, Massachusetts, brothers Theodore and Milton Deutschmann opened a retail and mail-order store that sold supplies for radio officers on ships and people who operated ham radios. They named the store "RadioShack," after a nautical term

for the small wooden cabin that housed a ship's radio equipment.

These two small enterprises would later converge and evolve into RadioShack Corporation, a multifaceted, multibillion-dollar company and one of the nation's largest retailers of consumer electronics.

Through the lean years of the Great Depression and the rationing of leather during World War II, the Hinckley-Tandy Leather Company survived and even grew. Dave Tandy's oldest son, Charles Tandy, joined the company in 1947, and his ambitions clashed with those of Hinckley. Unable to agree on the company's direction, Hinckley and the Tandys parted ways in 1950. Hinckley kept the shoe business, and Charles and his father formed Tandy Leather Company, aiming to capitalize on the growing leathercraft market.

Amalgamation of Interests

By 1954, Tandy Leather Company had expanded to 67 stores in 36 states and Hawaii. It needed to attract investors to sustain growth, however, so it was sold to American Hide and Leather of Boston, which then became General American Industries. But after a string of unsuccessful acquisitions, the parent company found itself mired in financial woes. Charles took control of the company in 1959 and was elected chairman. He changed the name to Tandy Corporation, and in 1960 the company began public trading (NYSE: TAN).

Meanwhile, RadioShack had prospered and grown. By 1960, it had nine retail stores and a profitable mail-order business. Soon after, though, the company fell on hard times, and in 1963 Charles Tandy, who had developed an interest in consumer electronics, purchased RadioShack.

By 1975, Tandy Corporation had become exclusively an electronics company. RadioShack grew tremendously over the next 15 years—not only in the number of stores but also in the breadth and quality of the electronics offered. Since then, RadioShack has grown into a national network of retail stores and support services, with net sales and operating revenues topping $5 billion in 2005.

Knowledgeable Sales Associates

RadioShack's highly knowledgeable associates are a core strength for the company. A leading consumer advocacy publication ranked RadioShack's sales associates at the top among retail consumer service providers, and NPD Group, an industry research company, rated RadioShack sales associates the best in wireless customer service and overall customer satisfaction.

Brand-Name Products

Responding to consumer demand for brand-name products, RadioShack created alliances with some of the best known and most trusted brands in consumer electronics and computers. Today, the company is the leading retailer of Sirius satellite radio and is among the leading retailers of wireless phones in the United States. In 2005 RadioShack announced long-term partnerships with Sprint, Nextel, and Cingular Wireless. In conjunction with these partnerships, it also expanded its wireless kiosk business.

RadioShack makes available additional information about its many products on its Web site (www.radioshack.com).

Throughout its rich history, RadioShack has built a well-earned reputation among consumers for superior customer service, comprehensive solutions, brand strength, and high standards of integrity.

Above: Many of the most popular and dependable electronic products available are featured by RadioShack at its modern stores, where sales associates are trained to help customers select the best products to suit their needs.

Frank Kent Motor Company

The remarkable success of this award-winning dealership is an tribute to its founder and his philosophy of 'a fair deal' and dedication to the satisfaction of each and every customer. Family-owned and -operated, Frank Kent Motor Company showcases Cadillac, Buick, Pontiac, GMC, Hummer, and Honda vehicles.

Above left: Frank Kent opened Frank Kent Motor Company in Fort Worth in 1930 to offer customers the best quality vehicles for the best value. He became known for his honesty and integrity. Above right: The original Frank Kent Motor Company Cadillac building in Fort Worth is shown here in the 1950s. Today the Frank Kent company has expanded to include Buick, Pontiac, GMC, Hummer, and Honda franchises.

Since 1930 the Frank Kent Motor Company has been satisfying its customers simply by adhering to the motto practiced by the company's founder, Frank Kent, throughout his successful career: "A dollar's worth of merchandise or service for every dollar charged." Kent's sensible and compassionate approach to selling earned him a great deal of respect throughout the Fort Worth community. His legacy remains intact to this day because of his superlative salesmanship and his consideration for the people around him.

The family company is now owned and operated by Will and Corrie Churchill, great-grandchildren of Kent. The Cadillac dealership established in Fort Worth in 1953 has expanded throughout the years and now also includes Buick, Pontiac, GMC, Hummer, and Honda franchises, serving the entire Dallas–Fort Worth area. Its loyal staff strives to build and maintain exemplary customer relationships, proudly carrying on the tradition of the man they admire.

A Fort Worth Start

It was a twist of fate that brought Kent to the automotive industry. A native of a small Missouri town, Kent was slated to join the family's successful clothing business, but World War I altered his plans. During a quick trip to Fort Worth prior to his enlistment, he was introduced to his future wife, Florence Mary Peak Jones, daughter of the first child born in Fort Worth and granddaughter of the first physician to be stationed at the newly established fort named Fort Worth in 1860.

Kent returned from military duty decorated with a Purple Heart for his valor during the campaign in Lyons, France. In 1919 he married Jones, and the two returned to Missouri to work in the Kent family business. In 1927 during a visit to Fort Worth, a friend at the Webb-North Motor Company offered to give Kent a sales position there if he could sell one car before he left. To everyone's amazement, Kent sold four cars that day. He had found his calling, and he immediately moved to Fort Worth with his wife and their one-year-old daughter.

Expansion and Success

Within the next few years, Kent successfully started and sold two automotive dealerships in Texas, one in Fort Worth, the other in Lubbock. The name Frank Kent became synonymous with value and honesty. His motto became legendary throughout Texas and national dealer circuits. From 1930 to 1953, the Frank Kent Motor Company soared and Frank Kent, the man, became Frank Kent, the icon. The Fort Worth community patronized his business due to his sensible and caring approach to selling, and their loyalty placed his dealership

in the Ford Motor Company's top 10 national rankings in three categories—total truck, parts, and labor sales.

Kent gave up his Ford dealership in 1953 when he was offered a Cadillac franchise. The combination of Cadillac quality and luxury with Kent's honesty and integrity created an ideal union. It was not long before the Frank Kent Motor Company earned the designation of Master Dealer from Cadillac, an honor that has now been bestowed on the dealership a total of 28 times.

Kent remained involved in the day-to-day operations of the dealership until his death in 1987 at the age of 92. He received from the *Saturday Evening Post* the Benjamin Franklin Quality Dealer Award (now the *Time Magazine* Quality Dealer Award), and he was posthumously inducted into the Automotive Hall of Fame.

Community Spirit

The Frank Kent dealership continued under the leadership of Kent's granddaughter, Wendy Kent Churchill, who joined the dealership in 1967 and served as its owner and president until her death in 2005. Each generation of leadership has remained true to Kent's philosophy of offering a fair deal, and the dealership's primary concern remains the satisfaction of each and every customer.

Throughout the years, the Frank Kent Motor Company has reached out to its communities, through Toys for Tots drives and sponsorships for Cook Children's Hospital and the Lena Pope Home. In 2005, the dealership raised 100,000 pounds of food for the victims of Hurricane Katrina by conducting Hurricane Relief Food Drive 2005.

Top left: Will and Corrie Churchill, current owners of Frank Kent Motor Company (above) and great-grandchildren of the company's founder, visit with Fort Worth mayor Mike Moncrief. Top right: The Churchills display some of their best selling vehicles, the Hummer H3 and the Cadillac Escalade.

In a business where 30 years is a long time, Toyota of Fort Worth—renowned as 'Fort Worth's Only Authorized Toyota Dealer'—has established a history of business excellence, deep community roots, and a tradition of giving back through good works and philanthropic contributions.

Top and above left: Toyota of Fort Worth features a new 13-acre campus and a state-of-the-art showcase facility. Above center: This dealership's climate-controlled service center features 42 service bays, an experienced staff, and Toyota Master Mechanics. Above right: Toyota of Fort Worth is the record seven-time winner of the prestigious Toyota President's Award. Proud of this record are (left to right) Sean Musser, sales manager; John Easley, general manager; Jeff Musser, general sales manager; Greg Shea, sales manager; and Craig Maynard, sales manager.

For more than three decades, Toyota of Fort Worth has been proud to be a partner in progress with its beloved home city and the greater Fort Worth/Dallas metropolitan area. Toyota of Fort Worth, its management team, and its employees are proud to work and live in the Fort Worth area, where they also contribute as key members of the community.

Overall, Toyota of Fort Worth attributes its long-standing success and positive reputation to its corporate ethic and day-to-day practice of treating customers with integrity and honesty, and offering value for their hard-earned money—that is the Fort Worth way, the Texas way, and the Toyota of Fort Worth way. Service, in addition to its top-rated vehicles, is the superior product that Toyota of Fort Worth sells.

Customers always come first at Toyota of Fort Worth, and that is why they keep coming back. In fact, Toyota of Fort Worth's customers have made this dealership one of the top volume Toyota dealerships in the United States and the "Number one Toyota truck dealer in North Texas" (according to the retail delivery registrations of Toyota Motor Sales, U.S.A.)

And in 2005—for a record seventh time—Toyota Motor Sales, U.S.A. honored Toyota of Fort Worth with its coveted President's Award, the highest award a Toyota dealership can receive. This prestigious award acknowledges a dealership's outstanding performance in every aspect of the business, from vehicle and parts sales to service and customer satisfaction.

With more than 13 acres filled with more than 800 vehicles, Toyota of Fort Worth is one of America's largest Toyota facilities. Brands include the full line of Toyota cars, trucks, vans, and SUVs, including recent additions such as the FJ Cruiser, the Yaris, and the new fuel-efficient hybrid vehicles.

Toyota of Fort Worth also excels in caring for its community. Every year, throughout the year, this dealership and its employees are active in community and charitable events, including supporting and financing education, Little League teams, Speedway Children's Charities, Happy Hill Farm Academy/Home for at-risk children, the historic Camp Bowie organization, and disabled-veterans organizations.

Toyota of Fort Worth is proud to be part of Fort Worth's history and looks forward to continuing its contributions to the city and the community in the future.

TOURISM, HOSPITALITY, AND ENTERTAINMENT

PROFILES OF COMPANIES AND ORGANIZATIONS

The Fort Worth Stockyards National Historic District

One of Fort Worth's treasures, this popular area is steeped in rich Texas history and brimming with entertainment options. From authentic Texas steak houses, western saloons, and specialty shops to world-famous rodeos, wild west extravaganzas, and stellar musical performances, this historical landmark has it all.

Above left: Stockyards Station, in the heart of The Fort Worth Stockyards National Historic District, features the country's only daily longhorn cattle drive. along with restaurants and shops, historic landmarks, and western entertainment —an exciting blend of new and old. Above center: Live professional bull riding is presented at the famous Billy Bob's Texas, "The World's Largest Honky Tonk," along with concerts by some of country music's best-known performers, an arcade, gift shop, and authentic Texas cuisine. Above left: Legendary singer-songwriter Willie Nelson was inducted into the Texas Cowboy Hall of Fame in 2005 and received the Rick Smith "Spirit of Texas" award.

More than 100 years ago, longhorn cattle were herded through Fort Worth and brought to market. Today the city, also known as "Cowtown," is celebrated and remembered as one of the most popular tourist attractions in Texas—The Fort Worth Stockyards National Historic District.

This collection of restored historic buildings are now authentic western attractions that capture the true flavor of the west and offer some of the best entertainment in Fort Worth. Twice daily the Fort Worth Herd of longhorn cattle are driven along the brick streets of Exchange Avenue by working cowboys dressed in authentic, turn-of-the-century clothing.

More exciting western action takes place at the Cowtown Coliseum (www.cowtowncoliseum.com), built in 1908; it was the home of the world's first indoor rodeo. Today Stockyards Championship Rodeo features traditional events every Friday and Saturday night, as well as special scheduled visits from Pawnee Bill's Wild West Show.

Western heritage is also highlighted at the Texas Cowboy Hall of Fame (www.texascowboyhalloffame.com), which honors excellence in competition, business, and support of rodeo and the western lifestyle. Personal mementos from more than 200 cowboys and cowgirls are on display, as well as presentations that pay tribute to famous western entertainers. The Texas Cowboy Hall of Fame also features the Sterquell Wagon Collection, John Justin Trail of Fame, Western Gift Shop, and Olde Tyme Photo Parlor.

Once a cattle barn, Billy Bob's Texas (www.billybobstexas.com) is now known as "The World's Largest Honky Tonk," sprawling three acres—and is in a class by itself. Honored repeatedly as the Country Music Club of the Year, Billy Bob's features the biggest names in country and rock 'n' roll music and can accommodate 6,000 fans. In addition to concerts, Billy Bob's patrons of all ages can enjoy dance lessons, professional bull riding, a celebrity wall of fame, an arcade, and a restaurant and gift store.

Stockyards Station (www.stockyardsstation.com) offers something for everyone. The old hog and sheep pens have been transformed into 25 shops and restaurants. There are historical walking tours along the Texas Trail of Fame, horseback trail rides, a western art gallery, and a turn-of-the-century steam engine.

Lodging is available at the western-themed AmeriSuites Hotel (www.amerisuitesfortworth.com), where the most modern upscale amenities are blended with an elegant ranch-style décor and down-home comfort.

Visitors to the Fort Worth Stockyards National Historic District will find an exciting place to shop, dine, stay, and play, and will see why people say Fort Worth is "Where the West begins."

This organization improves the area economy by attracting visitors to Fort Worth—one of 'America's Most Livable Communities'—through promotions for conventions, trade shows, and business and leisure travelers and by providing top-notch service.

In Fort Worth, history and tourism are forever intertwined. After all, some of the very first out-of-town visitors to Fort Worth were cowboys who drove enormous herds of cattle up the Chisholm Trail, the major route out of Texas for livestock. As the city grew, it attracted many interesting characters, from outlaws Butch Cassidy and the Sundance Kid to lawman Wyatt Earp.

Fort Worth's standing as the place "Where the West begins" is a major reason why so many people visit the city today. But that is by no means the sole reason: Fort Worth is one of the nation's most diverse cities, with an amazing collection of museums and performance spaces, world-class sporting venues, and wonderful family attractions.

It is the mission of the Fort Worth Convention & Visitors Bureau (FWCVB), founded in 1965, to promote the city as a premier business and leisure destination to a variety of audiences nationally and internationally, thereby enriching Fort Worth's hospitality industry and the community's overall quality of life.

In spreading the message about Fort Worth, the FWCVB reaches out to three major audiences: professional meeting planners, tour operators and leisure travelers, and the media. To meeting planners, the FWCVB stresses the city's central U.S. location, remodeled convention center and other meeting facilities, vibrant downtown area, and popular attractions. To persuade leisure travelers to enjoy a vacation and spend vacation dollars in Fort Worth, the FWCVB uses a wide variety of communication vehicles, from conventional advertising to online promotions on its Web site (www.fortworth.com). The staff regularly conducts city tours for print and broadcast journalists, resulting in features by some of the most respected publications and networks in the nation and abroad.

The FWCVB also plans innovative marketing events, including the "Big Drive of 2005," which was held in Times Square in Manhattan. The highly successful event featured the Fort Worth Herd and the Texas Motor Speedway and was picked up by the media from coast to coast.

All of these diverse efforts by the FWCVB add up to millions of dollars in economic impact for Fort Worth each year. As Fort Worth continues to grow and improve, the Fort Worth Convention & Visitors Bureau will be on hand, working tirelessly to promote this remarkable city of "Cowboys and Culture."

The Fort Worth Convention & Visitors Bureau promotes the city—the 18th-largest in the nation and a thriving center of commerce and culture. Above left: Fort Worth is widely recognized for its "Cowboys and Culture." Left: The Fort Worth Cultural District, just minutes from downtown, attracts visitors from around the world to Fort Worth. Its offerings include museums, such as the Kimball Art Museum, shown here.

history of Fort Worth and Tarrant County. Since it began well over a century ago, this club has figured prominently in the economic and cultural growth of the city.

Above: The Top of the Town, located within The Fort Worth Club, is one of Fort Worth's premier restaurants. Its private location on the club's twelfth floor offers a beautiful panoramic view of the city. Opposite page: The Fort Worth Club building stands as a historical icon in the west corridor of downtown Fort Worth.

The Fort Worth Club has hosted so many influential people and noteworthy events that the history of this private club mirrors that of Fort Worth itself.

In 1885, a group of forward-thinking businessmen envisioned a private club—a comfortable retreat from the outside world and a convenient place "for advancing the business interests of the city," according to the club's founders.

Originally chartered as the Commercial Club, the name changed to The Fort Worth Club in 1906. The club's first home, a three-story building completed in 1887 at the corner of Sixth and Main streets, was demolished in 1916 and replaced with a six-story structure. Within 10 years, though, the club outgrew this building and in 1926 moved to Seventh and Throckmorton streets, where it remains today. The Tower Building was added in 1976 to accommodate the club's growing membership.

Over the years, The Fort Worth Club has hosted the city's highest-profile visitors, from presidents and foreign heads of state to corporate chairmen and celebrities of all stripes. The club was where key decisions that shaped Fort Worth took place. It was at The Fort Worth Club that city leaders arranged to bring in General Dynamics (now Lockheed Martin), the city's largest employer; General Motors; and Bell Helicopter Textron, to name a few.

Today The Fort Worth Club features social, dining, and banquet rooms on its 11th and 12th floors, an extensive men's athletic facility on its lower level, and 21 hotel rooms divided between floors seven, eight, and nine.

Other private clubs in the nation may have comparable stature and heritage, but The Fort Worth Club is truly distinguished by its members, who preserve the history, tradition, and hospitality that have always characterized this unique establishment.

Compass Bank
Compass Bank
W 7th St
ONE WAY
BUS LANE
ONE WAY
Compass Bank
Compass Bank

Courtyard by Marriott–Fort Worth University Drive

Nestled in the heart of the Fort Worth Cultural District, this spacious hotel is designed to accommodate the particular needs of business travelers as well as leisure travelers alike, with guest rooms well equipped for productivity and comfort.

Above: Known for its customer-focused design, which allows guests to be more comfortable and productive, Courtyard by Marriott–Fort Worth University Drive is an ideal destination for both business and leisure travelers. Conveniently located within one mile of Texas Christian University, the Cultural District, and the Will Rogers Memorial Coliseum, the Courtyard Fort Worth University Drive is also less than three miles from downtown Fort Worth.

Leading worldwide hospitality purveyor Marriott International, Inc. is a company driven by strong core values and a positive culture. In the words of J. W. Marriott Jr., "Culture is the life-thread and glue that links our past, present, and future."

Marriott International operates more than 2,600 lodging properties in the United States and 64 other countries and territories. Its brands include Marriott, JW Marriott, The Ritz-Carlton, Renaissance Hotels, Residence Inn, Courtyard, TownePlace Suites, Fairfield Inns, SpringHill Suites, and Bulgari Hotels & Resorts. Marriott vacation ownership resorts include Marriott Vacation Club International, Horizons, The Ritz-Carlton Club, and Marriott Grand Residence Club. Marriott also operates Marriott Executive Apartments, ExecuStay corporate housing, and conference centers.

Marriott's popular Courtyard brand began in 1983, and today there are hundreds of Courtyard by Marriott hotels across the United States and in 22 other countries. Courtyard hotels are designed to serve every aspect of the business traveler's needs, and are also ideal for family visits, reunions, weddings, and vacations.

In Fort Worth

Courtyard by Marriott–Fort Worth University Drive provides superior service for any traveler. The hotel, near Texas Christian University, is nestled in the heart of the Fort Worth Cultural District, within driving distance of museums, theaters, sporting events, the Fort Worth Convention Center, Fort Worth Botanic Garden, Fort Worth Zoo, and more.

Newly renovated in 2004, Courtyard Fort Worth University Drive offers 120 deluxe guest rooms and 10 suites and features an outdoor swimming pool and an indoor hot tub and well-equipped fitness center. Recreational opportunities nearby include biking and jogging trails, tennis courts, and golf clubs. On-site, the Courtyard Café serves breakfast (only), with a healthy buffet and hot items cooked to order.

Each guest room features either a king-size bed or two queen-sized beds with deluxe bedding, as well as separate seating and work space areas. Special amenities include remote-controlled cable television with free Home Box Office (HBO) premium channels and pay-per-view movies, a hairdryer, and an iron and ironing board. Complimentary coffee and tea and a daily newspaper are provided.

Accommodating the Business Traveler

The Courtyard Fort Worth University Drive prides itself on being designed "By Business Travelers, for Business Travelers." Accommodating business travelers means keeping pace with their needs. Each guest room features a large work desk, two telephones with multiple lines, data ports, voice mail, and free high-speed Internet access.

The hotel provides a business library complete with data ports, computer printer, and copier. There are two executive meeting rooms designed to accommodate up to 60 people. With its customer-focused design, Courtyard Fort Worth University Drive specializes in making each guest feel comfortable and productive.

The Most Admired

Marriott's history began in 1927 when J. Willard and Alice Marriott opened a small root beer stand located in Washington D.C. The stand's business grew continually over the ensuing decades, expanding to include airline catering and then foodservice management. In 1957 the Marriotts decided to open their first hotel, in Arlington, Virginia, and through the decades, they opened and acquired many hotel and resort properties, initiating and building numerous brands. These activities continued steadily, and by 2004 Marriott International welcomed the 20 millionth guest member to its Marriott Rewards Program. In 2005 the company's holdings of 2,632 hotels and time-share units reached a total of 484,690 rooms. For year-end 2005, annual revenues totaled $11.5 billion.

Marriott International is headquartered in Washington, D.C., and has some 128,000 employees. It is continually ranked by *Fortune* as the most admired company in the lodging industry and one of the best places to work. It is also consistently ranked in *DiversityInc*'s Top 50 Companies for Diversity, *Working Mother*'s 100 Best Companies for Working Mothers, and *Latina Style*'s Top 50 Companies for Latinas to Work For in the United States.

Marriott supports the communities in which it is located and encourages employee participation in charitable organizations. The "Spirit To Serve Our Communities" is the name of Marriott's initiative to support building strong communities and enrichment programs. Marriott has also established Pathways to Independence: Marriott's Welfare to Work Program, and Bridges: Marriott Foundation for People with Disabilities. In its many charitable activities, Marriott focuses on working with other organizations and making the most of resources to solve problems and develop answers to community challenges.

Courtyard by Marriott–Fort Worth University Drive is committed to the same principles espoused by J. W. Marriott. He started with a simple slogan: "Do Whatever It Takes to Take Care of the Customer." For Marriott, caring for each guest begins with paying extraordinary attention to detail, taking pride in the property and its physical surroundings, and using creativity to find new ways to meet the needs of customers.

Courtyard Fort Worth University Drive offers a wide array of amenities. Above left: The hotel's spacious guestrooms combine comfort and functionality, from custom-designed comforters, thick mattresses, and fluffy pillows to high-speed Internet access, a large desk with conveniently placed lighting and outlets, and an ergonomic chair. Above right: The hotel's lobby offers a bright, welcoming atmosphere.

Renaissance Worthington Hotel

For business or leisure, this hotel offers Texas-style service, hospitality, and amenities. The only AAA Four Diamond hotel in Fort Worth, the Renaissance Worthington is centrally located in downtown's historic Sundance Square, making it the ideal destination.

Above: Located in the heart of downtown Fort Worth, the Renaissance Worthington Hotel is known for its impeccable Texas-style service and gracious hospitality.

Once regarded as a Wild West outpost, Fort Worth today exudes refinement, and the visually dramatic 12-floor Renaissance Worthington Hotel is one of the highest expressions of the city's sophistication.

Centrally located in Fort Worth's historic Sundance Square, the Renaissance Worthington is the hotel for discriminating business, leisure, and meeting guests. It combines warm, Texas-style service with modern elegance. Its expansive lobby, tastefully appointed with whimsical western touches, sets a standard for warmth and style. Nicknamed The Star of Texas™, the Renaissance Worthington is Fort Worth's only AAA Four Diamond hotel, and it has won this rating every year since it opened in 1981.

Meeting Needs, Exceeding Expectations

All of the Renaissance Worthington's 474 guest rooms and 30 suites are decorated in warm, vibrant colors and are classically furnished, with luxurious bedding that includes down comforters, custom duvets, and cotton-rich linens. Each room has a refrigerator, coffeemaker, hair dryer, minibar, VCR, and TV with cable and satellite.

To meet the needs of the modern business traveler, accommodations include in-room speakerphones, voice mail, and data ports, as well as a full-service business center, free newspapers (delivered to the guest's room), and toll-free phone calls. High-speed wireless Internet is available in meeting rooms and the lobby.

Creating Successful, Elegant Events

The Renaissance Worthington staff can make any occasion a success, from high-tech business meetings to casual receptions to black-tie events.

The hotel's 21 meeting rooms offer more than 57,000 flexible square feet of meeting and banquet space. The Grand Ballroom, which is 10,530 square feet, can be divided into five sections. An 11,000-square-foot terrace is available for outdoor receptions.

The Rio Grande Room, with more than 12,600 square feet, is the hotel's largest and most versatile space. It can seat 1,300 and accommodate large exhibitions or elegant wedding receptions.

Clearly, the Renaissance Worthington has the class and charm to create unforgettable events. The hotel offers the ultimate in catering and service, and even provides online planning tools for any occasion: a comprehensive event-planning guide, complimentary planning time lines, budgeting checklists, tips for promotion and publicity, negotiation techniques, and tips for food and beverages.

Beginning with the full-service business center, the Renaissance Worthington is perfect for business meetings. The hotel's full complement of audiovisual and electronic equipment, plus a staff of meeting specialists, ensures that each meeting goes smoothly.

Specializing in Relaxation and Recreation

The Renaissance Worthington is also an ideal place to relax and enjoy the Fort Worth area. It is steps away from the prestigious Bass Performance Hall. The hotel is also just a short drive from the Fort Worth Zoo and Forest Park, Billy Bob's Texas ("The World's Largest Honky Tonk"), Six Flags Over Texas and Hurricane Harbor, the Kimbell Art Museum, and many restaurants. The hotel's Kalamatas Restaurant and Martini Bar is ideal for meeting friends or colleagues, or just enjoying casual Mediterranean cuisine.

For active recreation, the Renaissance Worthington is close to golf courses, biking and jogging trails, and lakes for sailing and water skiing. The hotel also gives guests complimentary memberships to the Worthington Athletic Club, a state-of-the-art fitness center with Nautilus equipment, free weights, treadmills, step machines, and stationary bicycles. Guests can also avail themselves of the hotel's whirlpool spa, indoor pool, and tennis courts.

The Renaissance Worthington Hotel artfully blends style, sophistication, and a full menu of amenities so its guests can work, play, and enjoy Fort Worth.

Top left: First impressions are lasting, and the lobby of the Renaissance Worthington Hotel is a guest's first glimpse of the hotel's high standard of style and elegance. Above right: Spacious guestrooms are appointed with tasteful furnishings, rich colors, and western sophistication. Below left: Guests can experience a bit of the Mediterranean with authentic food and ambiance at Kalamatas, the hotel's restaurant.

Residence Inn Fort Worth River Plaza

World-class hospitality and comfort are offered in a residential setting at the Residence Inn Fort Worth River Plaza. This extended-stay hotel's contemporary decor, spacious suites, and round-the-clock service from its welcoming, responsive staff make every guest feel right at home.

Above: Located along the beautiful Trinity River jogging trail, the Residence Inn Fort Worth River Plaza—offering suites with spacious living areas and fully equipped kitchens—is minutes away from some of Fort Worth's best entertainment, shopping, and dining venues.

The most satisfying and pleasurable hotel accommodations address every aspect of a guests' lifestyle, whether he or she is preparing and sharing a meal, working at a desk, or relaxing and entertaining. The newly renovated Residence Inn Fort Worth River Plaza delivers that experience by combining a multi-functional space with the comforts of home. Every suite exemplifies the company's motto—"Room to work, room to relax, room to breathe"—and every employee delivers a special brand of hospitality that is appreciated by business travelers and vacationers alike.

Ideal Services and Exceptional Amenities

Guest services, including many complimentary services, are provided by the inn's friendly staff 24 hours a day. A hot breakfast buffet and coffee in the lobby provide a complete and convenient morning meal. The evening hospitality hour offers a relaxing social atmosphere that enhances life away from home. Guests will also appreciate toll-free phone calls, local restaurant dinner delivery, newspapers in the lobby, and safe-deposit boxes at the front desk.

In-room amenities are equally plentiful. Guests will find bedding with crisp linens, large mattresses, custom comforters, and fluffy feather pillows. Fully-equipped kitchens with all necessary appliances, cookware, and serving dishes, as well as a gracious table and chairs are also featured. Entertainment options include cable channels, satellite TV, and pay-per-view videos and movies. In addition, individual thermostat controls allow guests to set their room temperature for their own personal comfort.

Recreation is found as close as the Residence Inn Fort Worth's swimming pool, exercise room, and Sport Court®, or guests may choose to visit the nearby Fossil Creek, Iron Horse, and Whitestone golf courses. The Trinity River jogging trail, tennis and volleyball courts, and bike path provide further recreational opportunities.

Ideal Location

Sightseers, meanwhile, are kept busy with the area's many noteworthy attractions and landmarks—all in close proximity to the Residence Inn Fort Worth. There are the Fort Worth Zoo, Will Rogers Memorial Complex, Fort Worth Stockyards National Historical District, The Modern Art Museum of Fort Worth, and Fort Worth Botanic Garden.

Ideal Place to Stay

Overall, rooms at Residence Inn hotels by Marriott—including this Residence Inn Fort Worth—are 50 percent larger than traditional hotel rooms and are designed to provide extended-stay travelers with the comforts and luxuries of home as well as services and amenities that support productivity. Committed to guest comfort and satisfaction, the Residence Inn Forth Worth River Plaza welcomes visitors to the community by delivering outstanding service in an inviting residence.

TRANSPORTATION, DISTRIBUTION, AND WAREHOUSING SERVICES

PROFILES OF COMPANIES AND ORGANIZATIONS

BNSF Railway Company

With a vital role in delivering goods—from magazines to machinery to fresh produce to petroleum—worldwide every day, this growing company is building on its successes and long experience, capturing new business opportunities and developing new markets.

Above: In 2005, to better express its image as an innovative leader, BNSF launched a new brand and logo, as shown here on one of the 288 locomotives received by BNSF in 2005. The railway's intermodal business has led the company's volume growth. In the 10 years following the merger, international intermodal business accounted for 64 percent of volume growth and domestic intermodal business for 16 percent.

A decade in railroad time is but a drop in the bucket, especially considering that the beginnings of BNSF Railway Company (BNSF) date back to 1849. But the 10 years from the 1995 merger that created BNSF through 2005 were historic, surpassing previous watermarks. In 2005, BNSF led the largest U.S. railroads with record volume growth of 5.1 percent, moving more than 10 million units (freight cars, trailers, and containers)—an increase of nearly 500,000 units over 2004 and 3 million units more than 1995.

The formation of BNSF through the merger of Burlington Northern Railroad Company and The Atchison, Topeka and Santa Fe Railway Company was anticipated to have many benefits, including extended market coverage and operating synergies. These outcomes have not only been realized but far surpassed expectations. For example, in 2005 BNSF posted a record of nearly $13 billion in revenue, more than double its 1995 revenues.

BNSF, with headquarters in Fort Worth, Texas, operates a 32,000-route-mile system that stretches across 28 midwestern and western states and two Canadian provinces. BNSF transports a wide range of products and commodities, including consumer products (including cars, electronic goods, textiles, food, and tools), industrial products (building materials, steel, lumber, chemicals, and heavy machinery), coal, and agricultural products.

For some 160 years, BNSF has been delivering the finished goods and raw materials needed to build a nation. Today, the company's focus is on using speed, agility, and resourcefulness to help expand the global marketplace for goods and services.

The 40,000 people who work for BNSF demonstrate the tremendous value their rail franchise brings to the entire global supply chain by moving one-fourth of the nation's rail freight. In addition to having the right people, BNSF focuses on having the right resources. Every day, BNSF operates an average of 1,400 freight trains, using about 5,700 locomotives. Since 1995 BNSF has invested more than $22 billion to keep its physical infrastructure strong and increase capacity through expanded track, yards, and terminals and by acquiring new locomotives and advanced technologies.

BNSF also has the right routes, operating the industry's premier corridor between Chicago and southern California (2,214 miles to Los Angeles), and the route between Chicago and the Pacific Northwest (2,218 miles to Seattle). These routes are critical to BNSF's success as they allow the railway to offer some of the shortest and quickest links between major markets for the

movement of containers and trailers. Such intermodal shipments, which combine the unique characteristics and advantages of rail and truck, are increasingly important to BNSF's business. BNSF handles more intermodal traffic than any other rail system in the world.

BNSF also is a railroad industry leader in technological innovation. One of the best examples is housed inside BNSF's Fort Worth headquarters: the BNSF Network Operations Center (NOC). The NOC covers 45,000 square feet—the size of a football field. From this nerve center, BNSF dispatchers handle all train movements across the railroad, and power planners distribute BNSF's fleet of locomotives. Nine big (216-foot-wide display) video screens provide a ready view of the status of many railroad operations—from locomotive supply and on-time performance to weather conditions and fuel efficiency. BNSF also has in place technologically innovative processes that are easily accessible for suppliers and for all types of shippers in a wide variety of locations.

But BNSF considers that its people—team members who are progressive, vital, approachable, and resourceful—are what make this railroad an industry leader. There are about 3,500 BNSF workers in the Fort Worth area, at headquarters (located near the intersection of Interstate 820 and Interstate 35W) and at other facilities in Saginaw, north Fort Worth, and Alliance. BNSF's Alliance Logistics Park is an intermodal, automotive, and carload transportation facility. Of the 33 major BNSF intermodal hubs, Alliance is the fourth-largest, based on a 2005 volume of 573,000 lifts.

BNSF's presence in the communities of Fort Worth and the surrounding areas has grown since 1995 as many BNSF employees volunteer their time on behalf of charitable organizations. In addition, the BNSF Foundation annually contributes about $1.5 million to nonprofit organizations in the Tarrant County area. Some 75 organizations were served in 2005, with major donations made to United Way, Texas Christian University's School of Education, the Fort Worth Symphony Orchestra Association, and Texas and Southwestern Cattle Raisers Foundation. BNSF and its employees look forward to continuing to help make Fort Worth a better place to live and work.

Clearly, the future for BNSF will be challenging given the increasing volumes the railway anticipates handling. But with the right people, resources, and routes, along with a vision "to realize the tremendous potential of BNSF by providing transportation services that consistently meet customers' expectations," the railway is well positioned to take on the next 10—maybe even the next 150—years.

Top: More than 10 percent of the electricity produced in the United States is now generated from coal hauled on BNSF coal trains like this one. More than 90 percent of the coal BNSF hauls comes from the Powder River Basin, on the Wyoming-Montana border, which has the world's largest single deposit of low-sulfur coal. Above: The BNSF headquarters campus in Fort Worth consists of the BNSF Network Operations Center (NOC), four large office buildings, and an employee center with a cafeteria and fitness facility. There is also a Children's Courtyard childcare facility and a United Railway Federal Credit Union office.

Dallas/Fort Worth International Airport

A significant part of the economic engine for Dallas and Fort Worth, this efficient airport is committed to remaining one of the best and busiest in the world. Its building projects and long-term development strategies are designed to serve the region's growth, attracting enterprise and making the airport more accessible to all.

Above: The broad expanses of Dallas/Fort Worth International Airport (DFW)'s 18,000 acres afford seven runways overseen by two control towers, making DFW the world's only airport that can land four aircraft simultaneously. Half of DFW's acreage is used for airport operations, and the other half is maintained in its bio-diverse natural state.

Dallas/Fort Worth International Airport (DFW) is an impressive 18,000-acre transportation hub that is ranked as the third-busiest airport in the world. It is also ranked as sixth in the world by number of passengers, serving nearly 60 million passengers per year. One out of every 10 U.S. passenger itineraries that include connecting flights make connections at this midcontinent international gateway to the world.

With its vast property and wide-spread facilities, including seven runways, 12 landing approaches, and three control towers, DFW is the only airport in the world able to land four aircraft at the same time. The airport offers nonstop service to more than 170 domestic and international destinations and has six low-cost carriers offering service to major cities throughout the United States. DFW supports 268,500 jobs and generates more than $14 billion for the North Texas economy each year.

Cargo handling is another operation where statistics support DFW's reputation for excellence. Located at a shipping crossroads with superior air, road, and rail access to major markets, DFW handles an increasing amount of domestic and international cargo, which quadrupled from 1993 to 2005 to reach nearly 250,000 metric tonnes per year. The airport placed at the top of *Air Cargo World*'s 2005 Air Cargo Excellence Survey, which ranked airports based on performance, value, facilities, and operations.

Capital Development Program

With air travel on the rise, DFW has invested $2.7 billion in a Capital Development Program (CDP) that will position the airport by 2010 to accommodate the steady increases projected for domestic and international travel. The CDP is projected to generate a $34 billion impact on the North Texas economy and create 77,000 new jobs from 2005 to 2020. The "crown jewels" of the CDP that were completed in 2005 include the two million-square-foot International Terminal D, with an integrated hotel—the Grand Hyatt DFW—and the world's largest airport train, Skylink. Other CDP projects include supporting improvements for runways, aircraft parking areas, roads, automobile parking facilities, and additional initiatives to enhance the airport infrastructure.

The Terminal D Complex

The new international terminal, Terminal D, is capable of handling 32,000 passengers daily. It features 99 ticketing positions and a federal inspection facility capable of processing 2,800 passengers per hour. The terminal's 100,000 square feet of concession space offers travelers shopping and dining, including upscale venues, and the efficient eight-level parking garage has 8,100 parking spaces and a SMART Technology system that shows

which floors are full. Skybridges that link parking garages with terminals have moving walkways and are air-conditioned.

The Grand Hyatt DFW, conveniently integrated with International Terminal D, is accessible directly from the terminal, as well as from curbside. The 303,500-square-foot, 12-story hotel has 300 guest rooms and suites and also features ballrooms, banquet and meeting rooms, restaurants, lounges, and a rooftop swimming pool, spa, and fitness center. Built to serve a clientele of global business and leisure travelers, the Grand Hyatt DFW has a staffed business center and an in-house audiovisual company, and wireless Internet access is provided throughout. Comfort, convenience, and outstanding service are standard 24 hours a day in the customary Grand Hyatt style.

The Skylink automated people-mover system has transformed the DFW airport experience. Skylink carries passengers between DFW terminals and is one of the ways DFW is accomplishing its goal of providing passengers with flight-connection times of 30 minutes or less. Skylink's electric-powered, two-car trains are bidirectional and travel up to 35 miles per hour on an elevated dual guideway. Every terminal has two Skylink stations, one at each end—the average passenger wait time for a train is two minutes; the average ride time is five minutes. On opening day in May 2005, Skylink had the capacity to handle up to 5,000 passengers per hour per direction. Ultimately, when passenger demand requires it, Skylink will be able to transport up to 8,500 passengers per hour per direction.

DFW's CDP includes a multimillion-dollar public art program designed to celebrate the airport's world-class distinction and express the dynamic culture of the Dallas–Fort Worth metropolitan area. At the center of the art program are the interiors of International Terminal D and all Skylink stations. More than 30 local, national, and international artists were selected to design the artwork featured throughout these spaces. The DFW Sculpture Garden, located outside the Terminal D parking garage on the Arrivals level, features sculptures on loan from the Nasher Sculpture Center in Dallas.

Optimizing Energy Efficiency

DFW uses half of its 18,000 acres for operating airport facilities and maintains the remaining 9,000 acres in their natural state, reflecting the biodiversity of the North Texas region. DFW is a member of the Green Airport Initiative, which focuses on the smart use of energy, and an Energy Star partner with the Environmental Protection Agency (EPA). The airport has launched its own initiatives for its fleet of vehicles and main utility plant to reduce emissions. Most of the vehicles used on-site, including passenger cars, buses, vans, heavy-duty trucks, and off-road vehicles, operate on alternative fuels, a commitment that has reduced land vehicle emissions by 90 percent. The main utility plant's equipment and systems were upgraded with efficient technologies that reduce energy consumption by 77 percent during peak afternoon hours, while also saving $300,000 annually.

Further efforts to protect the environment were demonstrated during the construction of the Terminal D complex when a total of 355,000 tons of demolition debris was recycled into cement for airport construction projects. Also, excavated soil was used in the construction of runway extensions. For these and other contributions, DFW received the Alliance to Save Energy Star of Energy Efficiency Award in 2005. The airport's philosophy of environmental stewardship reflects its commitment to invest in the community's future and to help improve the quality of life of its residents.

Above: DFW's Skylink automated people-mover system transports passengers between airport terminals, helping them make quick and easy flight connections. Skylink trains are bidirectional and travel on an elevated dual guideway. Skylink can handle up to 5,000 passengers per hour per direction; the average passenger wait time for a train is two minutes.

Fort Worth Transportation Authority (The T)

Whether the mode is bus, van, or train, and whether the destination is a downtown loft or the other side of the globe by way of the Dallas/Fort Worth International Airport, The T is in the business of bringing people together.

Above left: The Fort Worth Transportation Authority—widely and fondly known as The T—is a major supporter of air quality improvements. Its primary fleet of buses, vans, and cars operates on compressed natural gas, and it encourages bike riders by providing racks on all regular route buses. Above right: Passengers at CentrePort Station, which is located near the Dallas/Fort Worth International Airport, board the Trinity Railway Express, jointly owned and operated between Fort Worth and Dallas by The T and Dallas Area Rapid Transit.

Catch a new commuter rail, just a short distance from Hulen Mall, that travels northeast through Grapevine and into the Dallas/Fort Worth International Airport. Or, hop a different train near the Texas and Pacific Lofts transit-oriented development on the southern edge of downtown for a no-hassle ride to a Cowboys game at the new stadium in Arlington. These visions for expanded passenger travel options across Tarrant County are part of a 25-year strategic plan developed in 2005 by the Fort Worth Transportation Authority (The T) to make public transportation more rapid and regional, and with more rail.

As the hub of one of the fastest growing counties in the nation, Fort Worth will likely see more dramatic changes in its public transportation system over the next 10 to 15 years than it has experienced since the creation of The T in the 1980s, when residents voted for the first time to support public transit with a dedicated half-cent sales tax.

Today The T is a regional transportation authority of the state of Texas, governed by a nine-member board of directors appointed by the Fort Worth City Council and Tarrant County Commissioners Court.

The T annually provides transportation to more than seven million passengers on buses; vanpools; vans for the mobility impaired; and the Trinity Railway Express (TRE), which is the commuter and passenger rail between Fort Worth and Dallas. With the vast majority of its buses operating on compressed natural gas, The T has been a leader in the use of clean transportation.

The T's headquarters office and operations and maintenance facility are at the Hershel R. Payne Transportation Complex at 1600 East Lancaster Avenue. The T also hosts many public activities at the community room of its Intermodal Transportation Center (ITC) at 9th and Jones streets. The ITC's function is to bring together major modes of passenger ground transportation in one centralized, convenient downtown location. In addition to The T's bus and TRE service, the ITC, as the city's prime transit station, serves Amtrak, Greyhound bus, Enterprise Rent-A-Car, and taxis.

The T is a major mover in a new era for the expanded use of public transportation in Tarrant County, which is projected to soon have one of the highest levels of traffic congestion in north-central Texas.

Richard L. Ruddell, The T's president and executive director, states, "The T is committed to partnering with the city of Fort Worth and the region to help alleviate increased congestion through the strategic expansion and enhancement of public transportation."

Fort Worth Intermodal Transportation Center

SELECTED BIBLIOGRAPHY

American Airlines Federal Credit Union. Press release. "American Airlines Federal Credit Union Celebrates New Branch Opening in Seattle, Washington," 2006. www.aacreditunion.org/about-pressrelease-sea-opening.asp.

"Attention, Tarrant County Drivers: Road Work Next 6 Years." *Fort Worth Star-Telegram,* April 2, 2006.

Baker, Max B., and Dan Piller. "Political Power Broker, Fort Worth Civic Leader McMillan Dies at 87." *Fort Worth Star Telegram,* May 3, 2001.

Baker, Sandra."Allied Buys Land for New Facility." *Fort Worth Star-Telegram,* November 16, 2005.

———."Developments to Close Out Edwards Ranch." *Fort Worth Star-Telegram,* March 20, 2006.

———."New Gateway: Urban Village to Rise at Entry to Cultural District." *Fort Worth Star-Telegram,* April 13, 2006.

———."Stockyards Hospitality: New Hotel Fills a Gap in City's Lodging Strategy." *Fort Worth Star-Telegram,* June 9, 2005.

———."Tower Developer Joins Museum Place's Team." *Fort Worth Star-Telegram,* May 16, 2006.

Baker, Sandra, and Andrea Jares. "Plans Confirmed for Condo Tower." *Fort Worth Star-Telegram,* July 18, 2005.

———. "Work Begins on Wells Fargo Site." *Fort Worth Star-Telegram,* October 11, 2004.

Baker, Sandra, and Anna Tinsley. "Mercado Has a Buyer: Owner of Former Town Center Mall in South Fort Worth Expects to Close on North-Side Property within Months." *Fort Worth Star-Telegram,* December 10, 2005.

Banks, Suzy. "48 Hours Fort Worth: The Best of the City in Two Days." *National Geographic Traveler,* September 2000. www.nationalgeographic.com/traveler/articles/1111_fort-worth.html.

"Beam Town: Fort Worth No. 3 on Fastest-Growth List." *Fort Worth Star-Telegram,* June 21, 2006.

Bennett, Andra, communications director. Fort Worth Chamber of Commerce. Interview and review of company histories with the author, April 19, 2006.

Boeckman, Chantal, company contact. Nokia. E-mail, May 10, 2006.

Bohannon, Randy, consultant. Texas Manufacturing Assistance Center. Phone interview with the author, April 28, 2006.

Branch, Alex. "The Barnett Shale: The New Breed of Roughnecks: Gas Boom's Dirty Work Provides Life of Peril and Profits." *Fort Worth Star-Telegram,* May 14, 2006.

Brown, Steve. "Several Retail Projects Landing at Alliance." *Dallas Morning News,* April 14, 2006.

Burgess, Michael, U.S. representative. Honorary summit chair, 2005 East and Southeast Fort Worth Economic Development Summit, June 3, 2005. www.publicforumin-stitute.org.

Cantey & Hanger. Press release. "4 Attorneys Recognized Among 'Best in America,'" June 8, 2006. www.cantey-hanger.com.

Carter & Burgess. Press release. "Carter & Burgess Acquires Day Wilburn Associates," July 5, 2006. www.c-b.com/news/story_news.asp?ArticleNum=598&type.

Cash America International, Inc. Press release. "Cash America Agrees to Acquire CashNet USA Online Lender," (press release) July 10, 2006. www.cashamerica.com/news.html.

Cash America International, Inc. Press release. "Cash America Expects Second Quarter Earnings Will Top Estimates," July 10, 2006. www.cashamerica.com/news.html.

Cash America International, Inc. *2005 Annual Report.* www.cashamerica.com.pdf/2006Narrative.pdf.

Claunch, Aleshia. "2006 Real Estate Forecast." *Fort Worth Business Press,* January 2, 2006.

"Construction Drives Values Up." *Fort Worth Star-Telegram,* May 16, 2006......

"Construction Fuels Big Gains in Alliance: Corridor Posts Double-Digit Increases, but Growth Slows Elsewhere in Northeast Tarrant." *Fort Worth Star-Telegram,* May 16, 2006.

"A Cool $160,000: Top Steer Brings Highest Price Ever a Year after Scandal Marred Results." *Fort Worth Star-Telegram,* February 5, 2006.

Cox, Bob. "Bell Building $31 Million Facility at Alliance Airport." *Fort Worth Star-Telegram,* March 25, 2006.

Daniel, David. "Operatic Heights." *Travel + Leisure,* March 1999. www.travelandleisure.com/articles/operatic-heights.

"Developers Plan 60-Story Building." *Fort Worth Star-Telegram,* December 14, 2005.

Dickson, Gordon. "Life in the Fast Lane: Creation of the Interstate System Transformed Nation." *Fort Worth Star-Telegram,* June 29, 2006.

———. "Toll Dispute Won't Delay Road." *Fort Worth Star-Telegram,* February 2, 2006.

Douglas, Jack Jr., and Mary Rogers. "Perry Richardson Bass—1914–2006: 'He Was a Legend. He Was a Giant.' Oilman, Financier Helped Change the Face of Fort Worth." *Fort Worth Star-Telegram,* June 2, 2006.

Estridge, Holli. "Hillwood Plans New Alliance Office Space: Heritage Commons II Will Add 120,000 Square Feet near Fort Worth Airport." *Dallas Business Journal,* March 24, 2006.

"Fortune 500: Our Annual Ranking of America's Largest Corporations." *Fortune,* April 16, 2006. www.money.cnn.com/magazines/fortune/fortune500/states/t.html.

Fort Worth Chamber of Commerce. *Fort Worth & Tarrant County Economic Report 2005.* Magnolia Media Group.

Fort Worth Chamber of Commerce. *Fort Worth Chamber of Commerce Economic Report 2006.*

Fort Worth Chamber of Commerce. *Fort Worth Chamber of Commerce Membership Guide 2005.* Magnolia Media Group.

Fort Worth Chamber of Commerce. *2006 Major Employers Directory: A Directory of Major Employers in the Fort Worth–Arlington Metropolitan Division.* 2006.

"Four Warehouse Land Deals Get Board's OK." *Fort Worth Star-Telegram,* April 7, 2006.

"Fuel for Thought: Mansfield Highway to Be Finished in Fall." *Fort Worth Star-Telegram,* March 21, 2005.

Fuquay, Jim. "NAFTA Part of Global Trend." *Fort Worth Star-Telegram,* January 5, 2004.

——. "The Purchase of Justin: Berkshire Known for Hands-off Style." *Fort Worth Star-Telegram,* June 21, 2000.

———. "Siemens Sells Dematic Logistics." *Fort Worth Star-Telegram,* June 15, 2006.

———. "Texas Is No. 1 Again in Drawing New Business." *Fort Worth Star-Telegram,* March 3, 2006.

———. "Trade Secrets: Hispanic Business Pioneers Leverage Skills into Successful Enterprises." *Fort Worth Star-Telegram,* October 7, 2002.

———. "2006 Largest Employers List: The Rise in the Area's Population Has Translated into a Booming Job Market, with Most Industries Hiring." *Fort Worth Star-Telegram,* May 1, 2006.

Garcia, Jaime, senior vice president and general manager. Leo's Foods. Phone interview with the author, May 5, 2006.

Gold, Russell. "Drilling for Natural Gas Faces Hurdle: Fort Worth." *Wall Street Journal Online,* May 4, 2005. www.dowjones.com.

Hamlin, Suzanne. "Journeys: 36 Hours/Fort Worth." *New York Times,* June 25, 2004. query.nytimes.com/gst/full-page.html?sec=travel&res=9c01e1db1139f936a15755c0a9629c8b63.

Hancock, Dain, executive vice president. Lockheed Martin Aeronautical Company. "Together, We Fly." Speech, North Texas Commission Annual Meeting, September 5, 2002.

Hart, Lianne. "Fort Worth's New Noisy Neighbors: Gas Derricks." *Los Angeles Times,* July 5, 2006. www.latimes.com/news/nationworld/nation/la-na-drill5jul05,1,2270009.story?coll=la-headlines-nation&ctrack=1&cset=true.

HealthMarkets. Press release. "A New Name for UICI: HealthMarkets," April 14, 2006. www.healthmarkets.com/home/media/press_releases/2006_Press_Releases/pr_20060404.html.

Hendricks, Paige, media contact. Healthpoint. E-mails, May 5, July 10-11, 2006.

Hickman, Holt, chairman. Hickman Group, parent of SCS/Frigette Corporation. Interview with the author, May 2, 2006.

Holland, Jaymi, media contact. Cott Beverages USA. Fax, May 9, 2006.

Howe, Aleshia. "Bell Helicopter Builds New Facility in Alliance Texas." *Fort Worth Business Press,* April 3, 2006.

Hubbard, Gregory, media relations. Bell Helicopter. E-mail, May 30, 2006.

Hunter, Joan, media contact. Fort Worth Transportation Authority (The T). E-mails and phone interview with the author, July 11, 2006.

Jones, Art. International Mobile Air Conditioning Association (IMACA). E-mail with attached document: "A/C History," June 11, 2006.

Kalinoski, Gail. "Hillwood Properties to Build Speculative Office Building at Alliance Texas' Heritage Commons." *Commercial Property News,* March 27, 2006.

LaHood, Lila. "Smooth Transition: Justin, Acme Building Brands Report Few Snags during Integration into Berkshire Hathaway Family." *Fort Worth Star-Telegram,* April 9, 2001.

LaHood, Lila, and Mitchell Schnurman. "Buffett Bids $600 million for Justin." *Fort Worth Star-Telegram,* June 21, 2000.

Landy, Heather. "All Moved In at RadioShack: Ceremony Completes the Transition to High-Tech Headquarters on Trinity." *Fort Worth Star-Telegram,* March 3, 2005.

———. "Campus Vs. Tower: New Corporate Buildings Are a Study in Contrast, but Companies Are Learning to Combine the Best of High-Rise and Campus Atmospheres." *Fort Worth Star-Telegram,* March 21, 2005.

Lankes, Lisa, director of corporate communications. Justin Brands. E-mail, July 10, 2006.

Lundsberg, Suann, media contact. Burlington Northern Santa Fe. E-mails and phone interview with the author, July 17, 2006.

Massey, Carol, media contact. Alcon, Inc. E-mails, May 11–12, 2006.

Okada, Bryon. "Cowtown Population Growth Leads Region." *Fort Worth Star-Telegram,* March 24, 2006.

"$151,000 Grand Champion Steer Fetches Record Price at Stock Show." *Fort Worth Star-Telegram,* February 6, 2005.

Pellecchia, Michael, Susan H. Schoolfield, and Elaine C. Cole. *150—Fort Worth: A Sesquicentennial Celebration.* Montgomery, Alabama: Community Communications, Inc., 1999.

Perotin, Maria M. "Healthcare: Providers Eye S.W. Fort Worth." *Fort Worth Star-Telegram,* June 26, 2006.

Piller, Dan. "Barnett Shale Drilling: Not Every Landowner Is Happy to Have a Drilling Rig in the Back Yard—the Good, the Bad, the Barnett Shale." *Fort Worth Star-Telegram,* May 29, 2006.

SELECTED BIBLIOGRAPHY

———. "Energy: Good to the Last Drop, a New Breed of Wildcatter Is Now Prowling the Permian Basin and Using New Developments to Extract the Area's Remaining Oil." *Fort Worth Star-Telegram*, May 22, 2006.

———. "Gas Drilling: Community Windfall, Leases Give a Boost to an Old Neighborhood." *Fort Worth Star-Telegram*, June 2, 2006.

———. "Justin Industries, Warren Buffett: A Good Fit." *Fort Worth Star-Telegram*, December 25, 2000.

———. "Natural Gas: Realizing Potential—Deal Highlights Growing Wealth in Barnett Shale Play." *Fort Worth Star-Telegram*, May 3, 2006.

———. "Oil Exploration: East Texas 1931–Dawn of a Dynasty, the Moncrief Fortune and Reputation Began in 1931 with an East Texas Gusher." *Fort Worth Star-Telegram*, January 22, 2006.

———. "Richardson Energy Firm Is Sold for $1.6 Billion." *Fort Worth Star-Telegram*, December 17, 2005.

Piller, Dan, and Mitchell Schnurman. "Civic Leader Justin Dies: Former Chairman of Justin Industries Served as Mayor and Promoted Western Culture in Cowtown; Stock Show Icon, 84, Led Push for Arena." *Fort Worth Star-Telegram*, February 27, 2001.

Poirot, Carolyn. "Ahead of the Beat." *Fort Worth Star-Telegram*, March 17, 2006.

Potts, Andrea, media contact. Williamson-Dickie Manufacturing Company. E-mail, May 15, 2006.

Ragsdale, John, vice president–marketing, and Andrea Potts, media contact. Williamson-Dickie Manufacturing Company. Phone interview with the author, May 4, 2006.

Rodriguez, Ernest Jr., executive and co-owner. Casa Rodriguez. Phone interview with the author, May 3, 2006.

Rogers, Amanda. "We've Got Our Justins On." *Fort Worth Star-Telegram*, January 25, 2004, Sunday Life.

Sanders, Bob Ray. "County Loses Great Man, Friend." *Fort Worth Star-Telegram*, May 6, 2001.

Schmelzer, Janet. *The Texas State Historical Association Online: The Handbook Of Texas Online*. Austin, Texas: University of Texas at Austin. www.tsha.utexas.edu/handbook/online/articles/ff/hdf1.html.

Schnurman, Mitchell. "The CEO Zone." *Fort Worth Star-Telegram*, June 26, 2000.

———. "Not Just a Pretty Space: Dazzling New Campus along Trinity River Also Intended as a Symbol of RadioShack's Management Philosophy." *Fort Worth Star-Telegram*, March 6, 2005.

———. "The Purchase of Justin: Sale Marks Success for Chairman." *Fort Worth Star-Telegram*, June 21, 2000.

———. "Terms of Tax Breaks Shield Investment." *Fort Worth Star-Telegram*, May 10, 2006.

Shannahan, Amanda, public relations contact. Ogilvy Public Relations Worldwide for Uniden America Corporation. E-mail, May 15, 2006.

Sheridan, Mike. "Lone Star State's Robust Economy Brightens Real Estate Sector." Reprinted article, Urban Land Institute, April 2006.

Smith, Jack Z. "Planes, Trains and Automobiles." *Fort Worth Star-Telegram*, March 12, 2006.

Southern Business and Development. Various issues, Spring 2004 through Winter 2006. www.sbd.com/Issues/Spring2004/Currents/Index.Asp.

"Special Report: 2004 All-Stars." *Fort Worth Star-Telegram*, June 28, 2004.

"Special Report: 2005 All-Stars." *Fort Worth Star-Telegram*, July 18, 2005.

"Special Report: 2006 All-Stars." *Fort Worth Star-Telegram*, June 12, 2006.

Stout, Ed, former president. Acme Brick. Phone interview with the author, May 3, 2006.

Taylor, Ron. Taylor Public Relations for Acme Brick. Phone interview with the author, April 27, 2006. E-mails, April–June 2006.

"Teen Gets $160,000 for Steer." *Fort Worth Star-Telegram*, February 5, 2006.

Texas Workforce Commission. *Tarrant County and Fort Worth-Arlington Metropolitan Area Data by Industry and Employment, Fort Worth, Texas*. www.twc.state.tx.us.

U.S. Army Corps of Engineers. "U.S. Army Corps of Engineers Releases Final Environmental Impact Statement (EIS) on Fort Worth Central City Project," January 17, 2006. Release No. CESWF-PA-06-016.

Wagner, Tim, media contact. American Airlines. Phone interview with the author, July 14, 2006.

Watter, Elizabeth. Marguilies Communications for Bimbo Bakeries USA, Mrs Baird's Bakeries. E-mail, May 1, 2006.

Wethe, David. "Fort Worth Emerges from the Shadows." *New York Times*, December 22, 2003. www.nytimes.com/2004/12/22/Business/22prop.Html?Ex=1152590400&En=Dc9ae8996aa1a54b&Ei=5070.

Williams, Nancy, president. Health Industry Council of the Dallas–Fort Worth Region. E-mail and phone interview with the author, May 18–19, 2006.

Wren, Worth Jr., "Churning Out Chow at the Rate of 550 Million Pounds a Year, Purina's Fort Worth Plant Is Far from Run of the Mill." *Fort Worth Star-Telegram*, September 12, 1994.

———. "Grupo Bimbo's Bear Witnesses Signing of Mrs Baird's Deal: The Mexican Company Plans to Make the Bakery's Fort Worth Headquarters Its U.S. Operations Base." *Fort Worth Star-Telegram*, May 19, 1998.

———. "Time Was Right for Shareholders to Sever Bakeries' Family Ties." *Fort Worth Star-Telegram*, May 19, 1998.

Web sites of various companies, government agencies, and other organizations were helpful, including the following:

Acme Brick, Adventist Health System, AIA dailyLead All Access (and smartbrief.com), Alcon Inc., Alliance Aviation Services, Alliance Texas, Allied Electronics, American Airlines, American Airlines Credit Union, American Association of Petroleum Geologists (Explorer link), American Hospital Association, Americredit, Amon G. Carter Museum, AMR Corporation, Andrews Transport Inc. (ATI), Arlington Memorial Hospital, The Ashton Hotel, Atmos Energy, Automation and Robotics Research Institute (UTA), Aviall, Aviation & Aerospace, Avomex, Baylor All Saints Medical Center at Fort Worth, Baylor All Saints Medical Center at Southwest Fort Worth (formerly at Cityview), Baylor Regional Medical Center at Grapevine, Beechwood Business Park, Bell Helicopter, Ben E. Keith Beers, Ben E. Keith Company, Ben E. Keith Foods, Berkshire Hathaway, Billy Bob's Texas, Bimbo Bakeries USA, Brite Divinity School, Bunge Corporation, Bunge Oils, Burlington Northern Santa Fe, The Campus at CentrePort, Cantey & Hanger, Cardona Foods, Cargill and Cargill Flour Milling, Carter & Burgess, Carter Industrial Park, Casa Manana, Casa Rodriguez, Cash America International, Inc., Cawley, Gillespie & Associates, Cenex/Harvest States/CHS, CentrePort Business Park, Chemical Lime Company, Choice Homes, City of Fort Worth, Clampitt Paper Company, CNNMoney.com, Coaster Company of America, ConAgra Foods, Con-way, Con-way Freight-Southern, Cook Children's Health Care System, Cook Children's Hospital, Coors Distributing Company of Tarrant County, Coria Laboratories, Cott Beverages USA, Country Home Milling, Crescent Real Estate Equities, C. R. Smith Museum, Dallas/Fort Worth International Airport, Dallas Morning News, Dalton's Best Maid Products and Best Maid Pickles, The Dannon Company, Defense-Aerospace.com, Delaney Vineyards & Winery, Del Monte Foods, DFB Pharmaceuticals, D/FW Hospital Council, D-FWmall.com, DFW Movers & Erectors, Doskocil Manufacturing Company, Downtown Fort Worth, Inc., D. R. Horton, Inc., DynCorp International, EFW Inc., Elbit Systems, Encore Acquisition, First Command Financial Planning, Fort Worth Alliance Airport, Fort Worth Aviation Department, Fort Worth Business Press, Fort Worth Cats, Fort Worth Chamber of Commerce, Fort Worth Convention & Visitors Bureau, Fort Worth Geological Society, Fort Worth Museum of Science and History, Fort Worth South, Inc., *Fort Worth Star-Telegram*, Fort Worth Stock Show and Rodeo, Fort Worth Transportation Authority (The T), Fort Worth Zoo, Fossil Creek (business park), Freese and Nichols, Inc., Galderma, Galderma USA, General Motors, General Motors Assembly Plant-Arlington, Gideon Toal, GlobalSecurity.org, Goliath Knowledge on Hand, Grapevine Mills, Halliburton, Halliburton Energy Services, Hallmark Financial Services, Handbook of Texas History Online, The Handbook of Texas Online, Hahnfeld Hoffer Stanford H&M Food Systems, Harbison-Fischer Manufacturing Company, Harris Methodist Fort Worth, HCA North Texas, Health Industry Council of the Dallas–Fort Worth Region, HealthMarkets, Healthpoint, HealthSouth Hospitals, Hillwood, Hillwood Development, Hillwood Group, Hillwood Properties, Hillwood Residential, Hoover's, Horizon Milling, Huguley Memorial Medical Center, Hulen Mall, Ibarra's, Israeli Association of Electronics & Software Industries, I-35W Coalition, John Peter Smith Hospital, JPS Health Network, Juarez Foods, Justin Boot Company, Justin Brands, Kelly, Hart & Hallman, Kettle Cooked Foods, Kimbell Art Museum, Kollsman Inc., Komatsu Architecture, KPR Foods, LaSalle Investment Management (research department CalEast Web site), Law, Snakard, & Gambill, Leo's Foods, LG Electronics, Lisa Motor Lines, Lockheed Martin, Lockheed Martin Aeronautics, Logistics Park–Alliance, Lonesome Dove Bistro, Lone Star Park, LoneStar Transportation, Main Street Arts Festival, Mark IV Industrial Park, MayFest, McCaslin & Company, McDonald Sanders, Medical Center of Arlington (HCA), Medtronic, Mercantile Center (business park), Miller Brewing, Mission Foods, The Modern Art Museum of Fort Worth, Morningstar, Motorola, Mrs Baird's Bakeries, National Basketball Association, National Cowboys of Color Museum, National Cowgirl Museum and Hall of Fame, National Semiconductor–Arlington, National Semiconductor Corporation, National Weather Service, Naval Air Station Joint Reserve Base (Fort Worth, Texas), Nokia, Nokia Telecommunications, North Central Texas Council of Governments, North Fort Worth Historical Society, North Hills Hospital (HCA), O. B. Macaroni Company, Oil and Gas Investor, Oil States Industries, OmniAmerican Bank, Partners for Livable Communities, PGA Tour, Pier 1 Imports, Plaza Medical Center of Fort Worth (HCA), Pulido's, Purina Mills, Quicksilver Resources, RadioShack, Rahr & Sons Brewing, Railhead Fort Worth (industrial park), Ranch Style Beans, Range Resources, Renfro Foods, R. Ibarra's, Ridgmar Mall, Riverbend Business Park, Roadway Express, Rodriguez Festive Foods, Sabre Holdings, Saddle Creek Corporation, SCS/Frigette Corporation, Shannon, Gracey, Ratliff & Miller, Sid Richardson Collection of Western Art, Siemens L&A Postal Automation, Siemens Logistics and Assembly System, Simeus Foods International, Simon Properties, Site Selection magazine, Southwestern Baptist Theological Seminary, Southwestern Carriers, Southwestern Petroleum Corporation, SPM Services, Sproles Woodard, State National Bancshares, Stevens Technology LLC (formerly Stevens International), StockHouse USA, Stockyards National Historic District, Sundance Square, Tarrant County College (Downtown Campus, Northeast Campus, South Campus, and Southeast Campus), Tarrant County Hospital District, Texas A&M Real Estate Research Center, Texas Boys Choir, Texas Christian University, Texas College of Osteopathic Medicine, Texas Department of Transportation, Texas Drilling Observer, Texas Health Resources, Texas Jet, Texas Manufacturing Assistance Center, Texas Motor Speedway, Texas Railroad Commission, Texas Wesleyan School of Law, Texas Woman's University, Texas Workforce Commission, Textron Inc., 35W Coalition, Thos. S. Byrne, Trans-Texas Corridor, Trinity Bluff, Trinity Industries, Trinity Railway Express, Trinity River Vision, Trinity Uptown, TXU Energy, Tyson Foods, Union Pacific Railroad, University of North Texas, University of North Texas Health Science Center, University of Texas at Arlington, Uptown Fort Worth, U.S. Army Corps of Engineers, U.S. Bureau of Labor Statistics, Ventura Foods, Vought Aircraft Industries, thewallstreetjournal/realestatejournal.com, White Elephant Saloon, Williamson-Dickie Manufacturing Company, Williams-Pyro Inc., XTO Energy, Inc.

INDEX

INDEX

INDEX

PHOTO CREDITS

Pages ii–iii: © B. J. Lacasse

Page v: © Michael Mulvey/*Dallas Morning News*/Corbis

Pages vi–vii: © Corbis

Page ix: © Douglas Mesney/Corbis

Page xi: © Doug Scott/agefotostock

Page xii: © Doug Scott/agefotostock

Pages xii–xiii: © Geno Loro/courtesy, Sundance Square

Page xiv: Courtesy, Cliburn.org/photo, Rodger Mallison

Page 2: Left, © Corbis; top, © North Wind Picture Archives

Page 3: © Corbis

Page 5: © Carolyn Brown

Pages 6–7: © Geno Loro/courtesy, Sundance Square

Page 8: © James Lemass

Page 9: Bottom, © Fort Worth Convention & Visitors Bureau; center, © B. J. Lacasse

Page 10: Top, © Harald Sund/Getty Images; bottom, © David Wilbanks

Page 11: Top, © Fort Worth Convention & Visitors Bureau; bottom left, © David Wilbanks; bottom right, © James Lemass

Pages 12–13: Top, © Dave Kozlowski; bottom, © B. J. Lacasse

Page 14: © Fort Worth Convention & Visitors Bureau

Page 15: Top, © Fort Worth Convention & Visitors Bureau; bottom, © James Lemass

Page 16: © Josh Moore

Page 17: Top left, © Dave Kozlowski; top right, © Dave Kozlowski; center, © Dave Kozlowski; bottom, © Fort Worth Convention & Visitors Bureau

Page 18: Top left, © C. Dewaun Simmons; top right, © Rick Lashua; bottom, courtesy, Six Flags, Inc.

Page 19: © Daniel James

Page 20: Top, © Donna McWilliams/AP; bottom left, © David Bailey; bottom right, courtesy, Fort Worth Cats/Bob Haynes photo

Page 21: © Fort Worth Convention & Visitors Bureau

Page 22: © Paul Wood/Alamy

Page 23: Bottom, © Robb Kendrick/IPN; top, © James Lemass

Pages 24–25: Top, © Corbis; bottom, © Dave Kozlowski

Page 25: Bottom right, © Dave Kozlowski

Page 26: © Dave Kozlowski

Page 27: Top, © Deedra Dedman; bottom, © Dave Kozlowski

Pages 28–29: © Jeffrey Hochstrasser

Page 30: © Rex C. Curry/epa/Corbis

Page 31: © Creatas/Inmagine

Page 32: Top left, © Keith Robinson

Pages 32–33: Top, Lockheed Martin Aeronautics Company

Page 33: Bottom, courtesy, Bell Helicopter, Sheldon Cohen photo

Page 34: Top, © Billy Brown; bottom, © Dave Kozlowski

Page 35: Top, © Rick Lashua; bottom, photo provided by Devon Energy Corporation

Pages 36–37: Top, © Ron Watts/Corbis

Page 37: Bottom, © Dave Kozlowski

Page 38: © Michael Prince/Corbis

Page 39: © Stockbyte Platinum/Alamy

Page 40: Top, © Bill Heinsohn; bottom, © Dave Kozlowski

Page 41: Top and bottom, © Dave Kozlowski

Page 42: Top, © T&L/Image Point FR/Corbis; center, © Doug Stocks
Page 43: © BananaStock/Alamy
Page 44: Courtesy, Harris Methodist Fort Worth Hospital
Page 45: Courtesy, Cook Children's Health Care System
Page 46: © Lise Gagne
Page 47: Top and bottom, © Dave Kozlowski
Page 48: © Dave Kozlowski
Page 49: Top, © Dave Kozlowski; bottom, © James Lemass
Page 50: Courtesy, National Farm Life Insurance Company
Page 51: © Dave Kozlowski
Pages 52–53: © Masterfile
Page 53: Right © Darren Greenwood/agefotostock
Page 54: Courtesy, DFB Pharmaceuticals, Inc.
Page 55: © Bryan Reinhart/Masterfile
Page 56: Top, © Matthew Wiley/Masterfile; bottom, © Dave Kozlowski
Page 57: Courtesy of Alcon, Inc. © Alcon, Inc.
Page 58: Top and bottom, © Dave Kozlowski
Page 59: © Dave Kozlowski
Page 60: © Dave Kozlowski
Page 61: Top, © Michal Bielecki; bottom, © Dave Kozlowski
Page 62: © Dave Kozlowski
Page 63: Courtesy, PNL Fort Worth, L.P. & City Place, Fort Worth
Pages 64–65: Top, courtesy, Trinity Uptown
Page 65: Bottom, courtesy, Trinity Uptown; right, © Dave Kozlowski
Pages 66–67: Top, © Dave Kozlowski
Page 67: Right, © Dave Kozlowski; bottom, courtesy, City of Fort Worth
Page 68: Top and bottom, © Dave Kozlowski
Page 69: Courtesy, City of Fort Worth
Page 70: © Jose Cantu/ Alwaysstock
Page 71: Top, © Paul Chesley/Getty; bottom, © Dave Kozlowski
Page 72: Left, © Premium Stock/Corbis
Pages 72–73: Center, © B. J. Lacasse
Pages 74–75: TRE, courtesy, Fort Worth Convention & Visitors Bureau
Page 75: Top right, © Dave Kozlowski; bottom, © Zach Holmes/Alamy
Page 76: Top, © James Lauritz/age-fotostock; bottom, © Jim Lopes
Page 77: © Dave Kozlowski
Pages 78–79: © Masterfile
Pages 80–81: © Christophe Testi
Page 83: Courtesy, Lockheed Martin Aeronautics Company, photo Ed Garza
Pages 84–85: © Marje Cannon
Pages 90–91: © James McQuillan
Page 97: © Masterfile
Pages 98–99: © Tomas Kraus
Pages 104–105: © Amanda Rohde
Pages 118–119: © Andrei Tchernov
Pages 132–133: © Ariusz Nawrocki
Pages 136–137: © Alvaro Heinzen
Pages 142–143: © Tomas Kraus
Page 147: © Photodisc
Pages 148–149: © Don Wilke
Pages 160–161: © Steven Collins
Page 169: Courtesy, Toyota of Fort Worth
Pages 170–171: © Todd Pearson
Page 181: © Jeffery Smith
Pages 182–183: © Bernd Klumpp
Page 189: © Justin Terveene

cherbo publishing group, inc.

TYPOGRAPHY
Principal faces used: Univers, designed by Adrian Frutiger in 1957;
Helvetica, designed by Matthew Carter, Edouard Hoffmann,
and Max Miedinger in 1959

HARDWARE
Macintosh G5 desktops, digital color laser printing with Xerox Docucolor 12, digital
imaging with Creo EverSmart Supreme

SOFTWARE
QuarkXPress, Adobe Illustrator, Adobe Photoshop, Adobe Acrobat, Microsoft Word,
Eye-One Pro by Gretagmacbeth, Creo Oxygen, FlightCheck

PAPER
Text Paper: #80 Luna Matte

Bound in Rainbow® recycled content papers from
Ecological Fibers, Inc.

Dust Jacket: #100 Sterling-Litho Gloss